The Happiness Flywheel

How to Achieve Success by Leveraging
Corporate Wisdom, Empirical Research, and Spirituality

Krishnan C.A.

Copyright © Krishnan C.A. 2025
All Rights Reserved.

ISBN
Paperback 979-8-89556-340-3
Hardcase 979-8-89632-972-5

This book has been published with all efforts taken to make the material error-free after the consent of the author. However, the author and the publisher do not assume and hereby disclaim any liability to any party for any loss, damage, or disruption caused by errors or omissions, whether such errors or omissions result from negligence, accident, or any other cause.

While every effort has been made to avoid any mistake or omission, this publication is being sold on the condition and understanding that neither the author nor the publishers or printers would be liable in any manner to any person by reason of any mistake or omission in this publication or for any action taken or omitted to be taken or advice rendered or accepted on the basis of this work. For any defect in printing or binding the publishers will be liable only to replace the defective copy by another copy of this work then available.

Dedicated to

My daughter, wife and parents for inspiring me.

This book is also a tribute to all my mentors and those

I've had the privilege to work alongside; our shared

journey has been the foundation for every page.

CONTENTS

ADVANCED PRAISE FOR THE BOOK

"Krishnan CA's The Happiness Flywheel offers a practical and insightful guide to achieving lasting fulfillment, going beyond temporary happiness. With a focus on mindset, resilience, and balance, Krishnan provides valuable strategies for personal growth in both professional and personal spheres. Krishnan's seven-part framework is both practical and deeply informed by his understanding of the challenges faced by professionals today. Whether navigating work-related stress or seeking a deeper sense of purpose, this book serves as an essential resource for anyone looking to cultivate a more meaningful and fulfilled life."

—Mohit Joshi
CEO and MD at Tech Mahindra

"In The Happiness Flywheel, Krishnan offers a fresh take on the concept of flow, guiding readers toward discovering their true purpose. His practical approach helps individuals align their passion with their work, leading to a deeper sense of fulfillment and lasting happiness in daily life. This book goes beyond offering fleeting moments of joy, providing readers with actionable steps to achieve sustained contentment and meaning. It's a must-read for anyone, especially young professionals, seeking to enrich both their personal and professional lives through purpose-driven living."

—Richard Lobo
Chief People Officer at Tech Mahindra

"Krishnan has written a very interesting book on the topic of finding Happiness and Fulfillment. His book offers an intriguing exploration of cultivating a purpose or goal-driven approach, developing the right mindset, and building strong relationships that result in a supportive team and create an environment conducive to lasting happiness. Along with these aspects, he emphasizes that the pursuit of happiness requires a certain level of detachment. By buttressing his arguments with quotations and real-life examples, Krishnan invites readers to join him in a shared exploration of these concepts, making the book both insightful and thought-provoking."

—S. Mahalingam
Former Chief Financial Officer & Executive Director,
Tata Consultancy Services.

"An absolutely lovely read for young and old. It is written in an easy unaffected way and is content-rich with life and work hacks. A simple observation the author makes, "By making consistent daily improvements of 1%, compounded over time, we inch closer to becoming 36 times better in a year's time." carries the qualities of not just being profound but imminently doable. All young professionals and aspiring executives will want to read this book."

—Dilip Keshu
Founder Born Group, a TechMahindra Company
Board Member at Reclaimz Inc and ProHance
Former Member of Board at Pininfarina and Saffronics

"I've known Krishnan for many years, and his book The Happiness Flywheel truly reflects his deep understanding of what it means to find joy in both the journey and the destination. By emphasizing resilience, mindset, and the power of relationships, Krishnan offers a roadmap that equips readers to build a life of lasting happiness, no matter the external circumstances. His guidance on developing detachment, a key to sustaining joy, is both practical and profound. The book presents strategies to maintain inner calm, even in the face of unexpected challenges. It's a must-read for young professionals seeking sustainable success and fulfilment."

—Pratik Pal
Former CEO - TATA DIGITAL

"Krishnan has addressed two audiences in one volume: professionals in today's hurly-burly world looking at a handbook for personal balance and contentment, and social scientists seeking a comprehensive reference on the science and art of human happiness. I enjoyed reading it, and so will you!"

—Ananth Krishnan
Former EVP and CTO - TCS

"I have known Krishnan for nearly two decades, and his unwavering focus on cultivating the right mindset is evident in every aspect of his work. His latest endeavor, The Happiness Flywheel, is a testament to this. The book offers clear strategies for achieving professional success without compromising inner peace, helping readers strike the elusive balance between ambition and contentment. It's a refreshing take on how to pursue goals while maintaining personal well-being."

—Rajani Seshadri
Co-Founder, IndePenn | Executive Coach |
Founding & Board Member - CII - IWN

"As a seasoned leader in digital transformation, Krishnan CA has helped countless professionals succeed, but in The Happiness Flywheel, he offers something even more valuable: a path to true happiness. In a world where success often comes at the cost of well-being, The Happiness Flywheel is a breath of fresh air. Krishnan's unique combination of corporate wisdom and spiritual insight provides a comprehensive guide to finding true happiness. His seven-part framework is especially relevant for today's professionals, offering tools to build resilience, foster relationships, and achieve balance in life."

—PR Krishnan
Former Executive Vice President – TCS

"Krishnan's book is an inspiring blend of timeless wisdom and modern insights, skillfully weaving the teachings of the Bhagavad Gita with lessons from top leaders. It offers a clear and thoughtful guide for today's youth, empowering them with a success code grounded in both spiritual and practical principles. This work provides a roadmap to happiness and achievement that resonates deeply in today's world, serving as a powerful hack for professional and personal success, as well as true happiness."

—Amit Bhalla
CEO, Hercules Hoists Limited (Bajaj Indef)

"Happiness is a state of equanimity amidst the antonymous journey of life: running after success on one hand and seeking contentment on the other. Corporate leaders and spiritual gurus play tug-of-war to epitomize that balance. Here is Krishnan, who makes it look easy and practiciable for the readers through this page turner…"

—Damodar Padhi
Former Chief Learning Officer – TCS

"In his book "The Happiness Flywheel," Krishnan C A explores the concept of happiness in a thoughtful and insightful manner. He challenges common misconceptions about happiness, such as the idea that wealth or career success leads to true happiness. Instead, he delves into the various aspects of what brings joy and fulfilment in today's fast-paced world.Krishnan discusses the negative impact of stress, the emotional challenges of modern life, and the fleeting nature of material possessions. By providing readers with tools for self-reflection, he encourages them to consider what truly matters in their pursuit of happiness.What makes this book stand out is its relatable approach. Krishnan does not offer a one-size-fits-all solution to happiness, but instead guides readers on their own personal journey towards fulfilment. "The Happiness Flywheel" is a valuable resource for anyone looking to gain a deeper understanding of happiness and how to cultivate it in their own lives. It goes beyond philosophical theories to provide practical insights on maintaining well-being and inner peace amidst the complexities of today's world."

—Arun Nair
Co-Founder and CEO - Learner Circle
Author of best-seller Murderous Greed

"Krishnan does a fantastic job of distilling ancient Hindu scriptural wisdom and combining it with modern science and strategies to achieve that elusive state of mind that we call happiness!"

—Jayaram Rajaram
Managing Partner - Bril India

"The Happiness Flywheel", by Krishnan, is an insightful guide for anyone looking to lead a more joyful life. From discovering purpose to cultivating resilience, the book covers essential qualities and practices for personal growth while also highlighting the habits that can hold us back. Filled with inspiring examples, anecdotes, and real-life stories, Krishnan brings these concepts to life in an engaging and relatable way. Even if you've come across some of these ideas before, having them all in one place feels like a friendly nudge toward a happier, more fulfilling path. This book is an inspiring resource for anyone seeking to enrich their journey toward lasting happiness."

—Ganapathy Sankarabaaham
Founder & CEO - Vajra Global Consulting Services

"The Happiness Flywheel, is your 'Wheel of Fortune' for a fulfilling and joyful life. Built on extensive research, simplified spirituality and corporate experience, Krishnan presents valuable guidelines and guardrails for breakthrough happiness."

—Mohan Kancharla
Independent Advisor & Author
'Consulting – A Practitioner's Perspective' &
'Design Thinking in Consulting'

FOREWORD

Happiness is a timeless quest that has intrigued philosophers, writers, and thinkers throughout the ages. It's a concept that transcends cultures, ages, and backgrounds, and yet, it remains one of the most elusive pursuits in human life. In "The Happiness Flywheel" author Krishnan embarks on a profound exploration of what it means to be truly happy, providing readers with a roadmap that is both insightful and practical. This book is not just a philosophical discourse but a guide enriched with real-life examples, cultural wisdom, and actionable advice.

From the very beginning, author Krishnan sets the tone by challenging conventional definitions of happiness. In our modern society, happiness is often equated with success, wealth, and material possessions. However, author Krishnan argues that these are merely superficial markers and that true happiness goes much deeper. It's about finding a state of contentment and peace that is not dependent on external circumstances but is cultivated from within. This perspective invites readers to reflect on their own lives and consider what truly brings them joy and fulfillment.

A key theme in the book is the concept of "flow," a state of being where individuals are fully absorbed in an activity, experiencing a sense of timelessness and intrinsic satisfaction. The author describes flow as the sweet spot where one's skills and challenges align perfectly, leading to optimal engagement and enjoyment. Drawing from personal experiences and a wealth of cultural stories, author Krishnan illustrates how finding one's flow can be a powerful source of happiness. This isn't just about doing what you love; it's about finding meaningful work that also meets the needs of others and provides a livelihood. The book offers practical steps to help readers identify their flow and integrate it into their daily lives, making it a central pillar of their pursuit of happiness.

Krishnan also delves into the importance of mindset and attitude. In a world that often emphasizes outcomes and achievements, the book advocates for a balanced approach where the process and the means are valued as much as the ends. This is encapsulated in the discussion on ethics and integrity, where author Krishnan emphasizes that true happiness cannot be achieved through deceitful or harmful means. Instead, a fulfilling life is built on a foundation of ethical behavior and respect for others. This message is particularly relevant in today's fast-paced, competitive world, where the pressure to succeed can sometimes lead to compromising one's values.

One of the most compelling sections of the book is the discussion on altruism and service. Krishnan argues that happiness is not just a personal journey but a communal one. By helping others and contributing to the greater good, we not only improve the lives of those around us but also enhance our own well-being. This idea is supported by various stories and examples, demonstrating how acts of kindness and generosity can create a ripple effect, benefiting both the giver and the receiver. The book encourages readers to engage in service, not just as a moral obligation but as a practical path to happiness. This perspective is a refreshing reminder that our actions have broader implications and that by lifting others, we lift ourselves.

Another significant aspect of the book is its focus on self-control and the conservation of energy. In a society where distractions are plentiful and temptations are ever-present, maintaining focus and discipline is more challenging than ever. Author Krishnan provides practical strategies for cultivating self-control, such as setting boundaries, prioritizing tasks, and avoiding negative influences. This is complemented by discussions on the value of simplicity and straightforwardness, advocating for a life free from unnecessary complications and deceit. The book suggests that by simplifying our lives and focusing on what truly matters, we can reduce stress and increase our capacity for joy.

The book is not merely theoretical but also deeply practical, offering a wealth of actionable advice. It guides readers through the process of self-discovery, helping them to identify their core values, strengths, and passions. It then shows how these can be aligned with their professional and personal lives to create a harmonious and fulfilling existence. Author Krishnan's approach is holistic, considering all aspects of life, including career, relationships, health, and personal growth. This comprehensive perspective ensures that readers have a well-rounded understanding of what it means to live a happy and fulfilling life.

One of the standout features of the book is its emphasis on the interconnectedness of all aspects of life. Krishnan beautifully illustrates how our happiness is intertwined with the well-being of others and the environment around us. This holistic approach to happiness is not just about personal fulfillment but also about contributing to a better world. The book encourages readers to think beyond their immediate needs and consider how their actions impact others. This broader perspective is both inspiring and grounding, reminding us of our shared humanity and the importance of compassion and empathy.

In addition to its rich content, the book is also highly accessible. The author uses clear and engaging language, making complex ideas easy to understand. The inclusion of cultural stories, personal anecdotes, and practical examples adds depth and relatability to the text. This makes the book not only a valuable resource for those new to the subject but also for those who have been exploring the concept of happiness for some time. The practical exercises and reflective questions at the end of each chapter encourage readers to apply what they have learned, making the book a practical guide for personal growth.

The book also addresses common misconceptions about happiness. For example, the author challenges the idea that happiness is a static state that can be achieved once and for all. Instead, happiness is described as a dynamic process that requires ongoing effort and reflection. This perspective is particularly valuable in a world where people are often searching for quick fixes or permanent solutions to complex issues. The book encourages readers to view happiness as a journey, not a destination, and to embrace the ups and downs that come with it. This realistic approach helps to set appropriate expectations and reduces the pressure to constantly feel happy, allowing for a more authentic and sustainable experience of well-being.

Another important theme in the book is the role of relationships in achieving happiness. Author Krishnan discusses how nurturing meaningful relationships, both personal and professional, can greatly enhance our sense of well-being. The book offers practical tips on how to build and maintain these relationships, emphasizing the importance of communication, empathy, and mutual support. This focus on relationships is a reminder that we are social beings and that our connections with others are a crucial part of our happiness. The book encourages readers to invest in their relationships, not just as a means to an end, but as an integral part of a fulfilling life.

"The Happiness Flywheel" is a treasure trove of wisdom, offering a comprehensive and nuanced exploration of one of life's most important pursuits. It is a book that challenges readers to think deeply about what happiness means to them and provides practical tools to help them achieve it. Whether you are at the beginning of your journey or have been exploring the concept of happiness for years, this book offers valuable insights and guidance. It is a beacon of light in a world that can often feel overwhelming and confusing, offering a clear path towards a more joyful and fulfilling life.

As you turn the pages of "The Happiness Flywheel" you will find yourself embarking on a journey of self-discovery and personal growth. The book is not just about finding happiness but about understanding yourself and your place in the world. It encourages you to embrace the journey, to learn from the challenges, and to celebrate the victories, no matter how small. Author Krishnan's message is clear: happiness is not something that is handed to you; it is something that you cultivate through conscious choices and a mindful approach to living.

In conclusion, "The Happiness Flywheel" is more than just a book; it is a guide to living a life of meaning and joy. It invites you to look beyond the superficial trappings of success and to seek deeper, more enduring forms of happiness. With its blend of personal wisdom, cultural insights, and practical advice, this book is a valuable resource for anyone seeking to live a more fulfilling and joyful life. Whether you are looking for guidance, inspiration, or simply a new perspective, "The Happiness Flywheel" offers a wealth of insights that can help you find your path to true happiness.

As you embark on this journey through the pages of "The Happiness Flywheel" may you find not only the inspiration to seek out what truly makes you happy but also the wisdom to embrace the journey itself. For, as author Krishnan beautifully illustrates, happiness is not a destination but a way of life—a way of being that can be cultivated through conscious choices and a mindful approach to living. Welcome to the journey of discovering your happiness, and may this book be a beacon of light guiding you towards a life of joy, fulfillment, and inner peace.

—**Dr. Saju Skaria**
Founder & CEO, Digitech Services Inc.
Phoenix, Arizona, USA

Prologue: The Pursuit We All Share

In every corner of the world, the quest for happiness feels universal. From the corporate executive chasing success to the student striving for good grades, everyone is pursuing something they believe will lead them to happiness. Yet, despite their achievements, many find themselves feeling empty or unfulfilled.

For years, I've been deeply fascinated by this. I've seen top leaders achieve incredible milestones in their careers, only to express a sense of incompleteness. I've witnessed students and young professionals burn out in pursuit of goals that didn't bring them the contentment they expected. Why is happiness so elusive?

When I delved into the plethora of self-help books on the subject, I found most lacked depth and empirical validation. They skimmed over the complexities of human emotions and the nuances of fulfillment. This realization sparked a journey of discovery for me—both through my corporate experiences, where I was fortunate to be mentored by some of the most inspiring leaders, and through academic study, including a course on the Bhagavad Gita at my alma mater, IIM Ahmedabad.

This book is the culmination of those experiences, a blend of corporate wisdom, empirical research, and spiritual insights. It is a practical guide to help you not only understand happiness but incorporate it into your life in a meaningful way. Across seven key elements—finding your flow, cultivating habits, avoiding the derailers of happiness, building resilience, nurturing relationships, seeking peace, and living a value-centered life—this book offers a comprehensive toolkit for a fulfilled life.

The chapters are modeled around Jim Collins' flywheel, a concept I admire for its emphasis on momentum and continuous improvement. Just as the flywheel helps companies thrive, the same approach can be applied to individual happiness.

I invite you to embark on this journey with me, as we explore the intricate relationship between happiness, purpose, and impact. Together, let's discover how to lead not just a happy life, but one filled with meaning, fulfillment, and purpose.

—Krishnan C.A.
krishnan.c.a2004@gmail.com
www.linkedin.com/in/krishnanca/
www.krishinsights.com

Introduction

Since childhood, I've immersed myself in countless stories and books, the familiar narratives that make up the fabric of routine life. However, one rainy day, with a cup of coffee in hand, I stumbled upon an old storybook from my college days. Among the touchy and hilarious tales, one story stood out, triggering the author buried deep within me.

The inspiration for this book stems from that intriguing story, a story that goes something like this…

Picture a wealthy man strolling on a beach, encountering a carefree fisherman lost in his world. Surprisingly, the fisherman isn't working that day, unlike his peers who've gone fishing. The wealthy man, curious, approaches and asks, "Why are you waiting at the shore while others are fishing?"

"Why should I go fishing?" responds the fisherman.

With good intentions, the wealthy man suggests, "You could catch a lot of fish, start your own fishing company, lead a luxurious life and make your family very happy."

Curious, the fisherman counters, "What if I already have a happy family who are content with me not working so hard?"

Despite the wealthy man's continued persuasion about the virtues of relentless work, the fisherman remains unconvinced. Frustrated, the wealthy man asserts, "Work hard, achieve material success, and then relax for true happiness."

The fisherman, looking straight into the businessman's eyes, calmly states, "Well, actually, this is what I'm doing right now—smoking a cigarette, relaxed, happy, and enjoying life."

Perhaps you've heard versions of this story, but have you asked yourself the same set of questions? How do we define happiness? What is happiness fundamentally? Is the fisherman's contentment in relaxation and enjoyment true happiness, or is the businessman's pursuit of wealth and subsequent relaxation more valid?

These questions compelled me to delve deeply into the subject, reflecting on the diverse perspectives each individual holds regarding happiness. But shouldn't we attempt to define happiness more clearly? And, once defined, how do we consistently achieve it in our lives?

This contemplation led to the inception of *The Happiness Flywheel*, a book that aims to explore the various facets of happiness, question traditional notions, and guide you on the journey to discovering and sustaining true contentment. Join me in this exploration as we navigate the intricate landscape of happiness together.

In my observations of the people around me, whether it's my team, peers, family members, or acquaintances, one thing becomes clear—happiness is not a constant state for any of us. The quest for true happiness seems elusive, and many of us find ourselves confused about how to attain it. There is no ready playbook or guide that provides a clear path to real and sustained happiness.

Simultaneously, the burden of significant work stress has become a pressing concern in our daily lives. The toll it takes on our health, leading to cardiovascular diseases and other health traumas, forces us to question the worthiness of trading our well-being for success at work.

Adding to the confusion is the common misconception that equates wealth to happiness. Yet, we see many affluent individuals not truly happy, while some people with fewer material resources lead content lives. Should we then associate happiness with success? However, even successful individuals often struggle with happiness.

It becomes evident that happiness is multi-faceted, with different grades and dimensions. How do we compare the joy of a beautiful child's smile to the satisfaction of receiving good grades in college? Material possessions, like a car or a house, provide a certain level of happiness, but it is often fleeting. Then, there's the profound and lasting happiness derived from love.

Before embarking on this book, I explored existing literature on happiness. While some well-known titles offered insights, none provided the depth and practical approach needed to achieve a permanent state of happiness. Spiritual texts, like the Bhagavad Gita, provided in-depth views but were often perceived as complex and challenging to understand.

Research works on happiness were also consulted, but they too presented challenges in readability and practical application. Most existing books either offered a broad overview, delved too deeply into a specific aspect, oversimplified the subject, or failed to distil information into a simple framework applicable to daily life.

Drawing from my personal experiences, reflections, and a synthesis of current happiness theories, I have sought to demystify the complexity of happiness in this book. It is designed to be an easy-to-read and practical guide, providing simple yet effective tips that can be seamlessly integrated into daily routines for tangible outcomes.

In summary, the pursuit of happiness is universal, and this book aims to unravel its secrets. Happiness cannot be defined by a single lens. To address this complexity, I have developed a seven-part framework in this book that examines happiness holistically and delves deeply into the subject. By fostering happiness and well-being, we can lead contented lives. Through this journey, I offer my best thoughts, simplifying the subject for the benefit of those seeking a stress-free life filled with energy and inner peace. I believe that, when applied, the majority of readers searching for happiness can find fulfilment and contentment in their lives.

CONCLUSION: YOUR JOURNEY TO SUPREME HAPPINESS

In *The Happiness Flywheel*, I've endeavoured to simplify the path and distil it into 7 key chapters. These chapters serve as steps that anyone can follow, guiding them from their current state to the supreme level of happiness. Each chapter unfolds a facet of the intricate tapestry of contentment, offering practical insights and actionable tips.

Let's briefly explore the roadmap.

CHAPTER 1: FINDING YOUR FLOW AND DOING YOUR DUTY

In the opening chapter, you explore the fundamental dimension of discovering happiness through purpose and achieving a state of joy, commonly referred to as "flow". Imagine a state of intense focus on a particular task, where distractions and worries fade away, allowing you to experience happiness consistently throughout the day.

The chapter argues that finding your flow is crucial for a fulfilling life, emphasising the need for you to identify something meaningful and invest energy into accomplishing specific goals. Picture engrossing activities, such as watching a captivating cricket match, where you become deeply involved in a task and experience a sense of enjoyment, with time passing unnoticed.

A central theme is the idea that meaningful engagement in life is the starting point for the pursuit of happiness. By immersing yourself in a purposeful life, distractions lose their impact, allowing you to experience the state of flow. The chapter concludes by highlighting the importance of your efforts in accomplishing goals, providing insights into finding your flow and mission in life, and offering practical tips for your journey towards sustained happiness.

Ultimately, the goal by the end of the chapter is for you to gain a comprehensive understanding of where you can find your own flow, setting the stage for a fulfilling and purpose-driven life.

> *"Those who can laugh without cause have either found the true meaning of happiness or have gone stark raving mad."*
>
> —**Norm Papernick**

CHAPTER 2: THE ENDS DON'T JUSTIFY THE MEANS. DEVELOPING THE RIGHT MINDSET DOES

In the second chapter, we delve deeper into a critical aspect of goal pursuit: the idea that the ends don't justify the means. Often, individuals become so fixated on their objectives that they are willing to do whatever it takes to achieve them. However, I've observed that such a path is not sustainable and can erode peace of mind over time.

Many find themselves mentally hassled and frustrated, leading to an unhappy state of mind that compromises their inner serenity and overall happiness. It becomes apparent that in the relentless pursuit of success, individuals risk losing the very essence of life. While the temptation to achieve success is strong, maintaining the right attitude and mindset is crucial.

This chapter explores the significance of developing the right attitude and mindset to pursue goals without sacrificing one's peace and joy. I delve into strategies that allow individuals to pursue their goals aggressively without compromising their values. The focus is on striking a balance between achieving objectives and preserving one's mental well-being. This chapter is also important as it addresses work-life balance and the development of the right attitudes to ensure that this balance is maintained while you pursue your goals with steadfast focus.

It emphasises the significance of aligning your professional ambitions with personal well-being, thereby fostering a harmonious and fulfilling life.

So, how should you go about developing the right attitude and creating a pathway that aligns with your goals without compromising your values? This chapter offers insights and practical guidance on navigating this delicate balance, ensuring that the pursuit of success doesn't come at the expense of your inner peace and happiness.

CHAPTER 3: AVOIDING THE PRACTICES THAT DERAIL HAPPINESS

Chapter 3 delves into the crucial topic of avoiding practices that can derail your happiness, even when you have the right attitude and a strong goal. It's a common observation that individuals, despite having the perfect mindset, engage in behaviours that hinder their happiness, leaving them somewhat discontent.

Even those intensely focused on their goals can lose their precious happiness and wear a smile on their faces as they navigate the path to success. Often, a negative approach towards life and constant complaining become derailing practices.

This chapter takes a detailed look at these detrimental behaviours that you should consciously avoid. It sheds light on the specific practices that may compromise your happiness, and if you find yourself demonstrating such behaviours, it provides concrete steps you can take to steer clear of these harmful hindrances in your life.

By the end of this chapter, you will gain valuable insights into recognising and eliminating practices that could potentially undermine your happiness, allowing you to maintain a positive and fulfilling journey towards your goals.

CHAPTER 4: TAKING OTHERS ALONG AND CREATING STRONG RELATIONSHIPS TO HELP YOU IN YOUR QUEST

In Chapter 4, we delve into the fundamental aspect of building strong relationships, recognising that achieving your goals is not a solitary journey. While individual success is a worthy pursuit, the elation and sense of accomplishment are amplified when you have a network of people cheering and supporting you along the way.

It becomes evident that building strong relationships is crucial, yet many individuals, in their pursuit of success, inadvertently burn bridges and strain connections. This behaviour not only derails happiness, but also creates challenges later in life. Unfortunately, by the time people realise these mistakes, it's often too late to rectify them.

This chapter delves deeper into the importance of building and nurturing strong relationships. I explore how to avoid the pitfalls of damaging connections in the quest for success and instead leverage relationships to achieve your goals. Recognising that true happiness is intertwined with the quality of your connections, I provide insights and practical tips on fostering and utilising relationships for your overall well-being and success.

By the end of this chapter, you'll have a deeper understanding of the significance of strong relationships in your quest for true happiness and how to cultivate and leverage these connections effectively.

CHAPTER 5: DEVELOPING DETACHMENT AND RESILIENCE

In Chapter 5, we delve into the crucial theme of developing detachment and resilience, recognising that even with a strong goal, a supportive team, and the right mindset, life is inevitably prone to presenting unforeseen challenges. These challenges, such as accidents, health crises, or sudden job loss, can be hard to explain and often leave individuals feeling helpless and dejected.

The chapter addresses the question: "How does one develop resilience and a sense of detachment?" These qualities are deemed essential for achieving long-term, sustainable happiness. It becomes clear that having a sense of detachment is imperative for maintaining mental peace and cultivating an aura of happiness.

I explore in detail the strategies and mindset shifts needed to develop resilience in the face of unexpected events. The goal is to equip you with the tools to navigate life's uncertainties without letting them compromise your inner peace and overall well-being. By the end of this chapter, you'll gain insights into the importance of cultivating resilience and detachment, essential qualities for sustaining happiness despite the inevitable challenges life may throw your way.

CHAPTER 6: FINDING BALANCE AND PEACE

Chapter 6 tackles the pivotal question of creating a resilient framework in your life to maintain peace of mind, even in adversity. It focuses on defining higher levels of happiness, aiming for a state beyond the harmony and contentment discussed in earlier chapters.

While the preceding chapters guide you through achieving happiness, this chapter elevates the discussion to advanced states of contentment and serenity. This heightened state of mind is characterised by complete peace, rendering external incidents powerless to impact your inner state.

The chapter explores strategies and practices essential for attaining this advanced state and experiencing tranquillity. It provides insights into creating a framework that withstands challenges, ensuring that, even when everything seems to go wrong, you can maintain inner equilibrium.

By the end of this chapter, you will gain a deeper understanding of how to achieve a resilient state of mind and enter a realm that transcends the earlier stages of happiness discussed in the book.

CHAPTER 7: QUALITIES THAT DEFINE A HAPPY LIFE

In this final chapter, let's explore the qualities that define a happy life. I'll guide you through essential qualities demonstrated by happy individuals and discuss their significance in cultivating true happiness.

We'll delve into qualities like fearlessness, honesty, straightforwardness, and the importance of being truthful to yourself. These qualities play a crucial role in supporting your quest for genuine happiness.

This chapter draws a connection with a famous chapter from the Bhagavad Gita, providing an in-depth exploration of the enumerated qualities. It offers a checklist of these qualities that need to be ingrained in your life to achieve a state of bliss and contentment. By the end of this chapter, you'll have a comprehensive understanding of the qualities that define a happy life and how to cultivate them for lasting fulfilment.

"HOW DO YOU USE THIS BOOK?"

You might wonder, "How do I use this book effectively?"

Young professionals can use the ideas shared in this book as a go-to guide and readily leverage what I learned from various leaders working in top organisations such as Tata Consultancy Services and the Mahindra Group. It also simplifies my interest in empirical research on happiness, which I have detailed in the appendix. At the Indian Institute of Management, Ahmedabad, my alma mater, a lecture on applying the Bhagavad Gita in modern life, especially in the corporate world, inspired me to study the text in more detail. I have simplified these learnings for young professionals to incorporate them into their careers and succeed in their chosen paths.

Once you've gained insights into the tools and frameworks presented in this book, consider trying out the ideas that resonate with your life. Experiment with those relevant to your journey, witnessing the gradual transformation they bring. Not every idea may directly apply to you, and that's perfectly fine. I encourage you to selectively embrace the concepts that resonate, while leaving behind what doesn't align with your unique path.

May this book serve as a practical guide for you to apply daily, paving the way towards the contentment you seek. I hope it offers numerous insights into your pursuit of happiness, turning it into a journey of self-discovery.

As you embark on this practical guide, I sincerely wish you to reach the pinnacle of happiness, redeem it, and sustain it throughout your life. Thank you for being a part of this journey.

CHAPTER 1

Achieving Your State of Flow and Finding Your Purpose in Life

INTRODUCTION:

On my first trip to the US, attempting to assemble IKEA furniture—what should have been a straightforward task quickly turned into a personal battle of wits with a set of screws and a very cryptic instruction manual. At some point, as I struggled to align the parts, I found myself wondering, "Is this really my purpose in life?" But it got me thinking: isn't life a bit like IKEA furniture? It can feel a bit disjointed and frustrating until you find the purpose that holds everything together.

Welcome to the exploration of the fundamental building block of happiness: finding purpose in life. It's the cornerstone that transforms a mere existence into a meaningful journey worth living, or, as some might say, worth dying for.

In my encounters with people, I've observed that many are yet to discover something truly meaningful in their lives. The relentless pursuit of happiness in material possessions, I've come to realise, is a futile endeavour. Material comfort and wealth, while valuable, become meaningless without a sense of purpose. True happiness lies in having a life filled with purpose.

Before we delve deeper, let's discuss a crucial concept – the concept of flow. Flow is that sublime feeling you experience when engrossed in a book or captivated by a movie, a state where time seems to slip away effortlessly. It occurs when you are doing something you love, something that captivates you, leaving no room for boredom. This extended engagement in an activity you cherish leads to a feeling of pure bliss, where happiness is abundant and fatigue is absent. This is the state of flow.

However, achieving flow doesn't equate to perpetual happiness. True and sustained happiness emerges when your activities align with what the world needs, what you love, and what you are good at, all while being compensated for your efforts. This intricate balance, as illustrated in the book Ikigai, is the convergence of what you love, what you are good at, what the world needs, and what you can be paid for. In Japanese terms, this is the realisation of your Ikigai, your purpose.

So, as we navigate through this chapter, reflect on what truly brings you joy, what activities captivate you, and how you can align these passions with the needs of the world. It's a journey towards achieving your state of flow and discovering a purpose that not only fulfils you but contributes to the world around you. Let's embark on this journey together.

According to Owen Schaffer's model, achieving flow involves a systematic approach. Let's integrate these steps into our quest for finding flow.

Step 1: Knowing What to Do

The journey begins with finding flow in the task at hand. A key strategy for this is rejecting multitasking, a pervasive habit in today's smartphone-driven world. Studies have linked smartphone addiction to increased feelings of depression and reduced community attachment. To counter this, we can employ techniques like the Pomodoro technique—25 minutes of focused work followed by a 5-minute break. Eliminating technological distractions, such as constant email checking, is another crucial step to maintain focus on a specific task.

Step 2: Knowing How to Do It

The second crucial step involves improving our performance incrementally with each task. Striking the right balance is essential—tasks that are too easy or too difficult hinder the achievement of flow. Consistently aiming to do each task a little better than before fosters a sense of concentration and flow in our day-to-day activities.

Step 3: Knowing How Well You Are Doing

Clear goals are the third key ingredient for achieving flow. Managers often fail to provide clear goals to their teams, leading to dissatisfaction and lack of enthusiasm. Having a compass-like clarity over an overly detailed map is vital. Team members need to understand the general direction (compass) and the ultimate goal (map) to cultivate a sense of purpose and a clear objective.

Incorporating these steps into our daily lives sets the foundation for finding flow. As we navigate through the intricacies of tasks, maintaining focus, continuously improving, and having clear goals will propel us towards a state of concentration and flow. In this chapter, we'll further explore and refine these principles, unlocking the potential for sustained happiness. Get ready to embark on this transformative journey.

FALLING IN LOVE WITH THE WORK

As the saying goes, "If you love what you do, work doesn't seem like work," encapsulates the essence of falling in love with your work. When your passion becomes your profession, you're essentially getting paid to do what you love. This perspective serves as a valuable framework to assess whether the work we engage in truly consumes us, and it aligns seamlessly with the concept of achieving flow.

Flow is an elusive state, nearly impossible to attain when the task is mundane or lacks endearment. The key to falling in love with your work is to question the larger purpose of the task at hand. There's a profound story I once came across that beautifully illustrates this point. A man observes a stonecutter happily carving a stone and, intrigued, he approaches and asks, "Why do you put so much effort into cutting the stone, and what is motivating about it?" The stonecutter looks at him and replies, "For you, it might seem like I am cutting a stone, but for me, I am building a cathedral. And that is very motivating for me."

This story emphasises that the stonecutter found purpose in his work – a purpose larger than the physical act of cutting a stone. Mentally, he was engrossed in building a cathedral. This perspective transforms a seemingly mundane task into a meaningful endeavour.

For leaders and managers in corporate settings, this story holds a critical lesson. It prompts us to ask ourselves, "Are we providing our teams with a sense of purpose, informing them about the larger goals?" If the answer is yes, we are on the right path; if not, it's crucial to communicate the larger purpose to motivate and engage the team. Take the example of building a satellite—each person involved, even in the manufacturing of tiny parts, would be more motivated and feel honoured to contribute if they understand the larger purpose of the project.

Even if you haven't yet reached a leadership position, consider how you can contribute to the larger purpose of the organisation and how it benefits customers and users. Clarity on the broader impact of your work brings renewed motivation and a deeper connection to the tasks at hand.

HEALTHY MIND, HEALTHY BODY

In the pursuit of happiness, there's a timeless adage that resonates profoundly: "Health is Wealth." It's a phrase we've all heard, but its essence is often overshadowed in today's fast-paced lifestyle. Amidst our endeavours to discover our purpose and understand what truly consumes us, the importance of focusing on our health should not be neglected.

A healthy body is integral to overall well-being and happiness. Imagine trying to navigate the complexities of life with an ailing body – it becomes an uphill battle. Therefore, as we invest in our mental well-being, understanding our purpose and finding tasks that truly consume us, it's equally imperative to prioritise the health of our bodies.

Regular exercise, meditation, walking, and a balanced, healthy diet contribute significantly to maintaining a healthy body, which, in turn, fosters a healthy mind. Scientific research has consistently demonstrated the interconnectedness of physical and mental well-being. A sound body not only boosts our immune system and energy levels, but also enhances our resilience to stress.

The demands of our daily lives, especially in the face of stress and high workloads, become more manageable when our bodies are in good health. It's an intricate dance, a harmonious interplay between a healthy mind and a healthy body, that paves the way for sustained happiness.

As we progress through this journey, exploring the facets of happiness and purpose, let's not overlook the simple yet profound truth that nurturing our bodies is an indispensable part of the equation.

The saying "Health is Wealth" has taken on a deeper resonance in my own life, especially with the recent loss of my father to a sudden and unexpected heart attack. Despite appearing to be in the peak of health, we discovered, to our shock, that he had a triple vessel block. His battle over the last 45 days in the critical care ICU, where the best of medicine and healthcare proved insufficient, was a traumatic experience for our family. A man who seemed destined for another decade of life faced an unforeseen and insurmountable challenge.

This personal tragedy reinforced the profound truth that focusing on health is not a cliché, but an absolute foundation for happiness and well-being. The fragility of life became glaringly evident, highlighting the crucial need to prioritise our health. While we delve into the complexities of purpose, flow, and happiness, let this serve as a poignant reminder that a healthy body is the bedrock upon which our pursuits stand.

> *"Happiness always looks small while you hold it in your hands, but let it go and you learn at once how big and precious it is."*
>
> **—Maxim Gorky**

CHOOSE A MISSION THAT SERVES THE COMMUNITY

As we navigate the intricacies of finding purpose and happiness, we circle back to the profound concept of choosing a mission that serves the larger community. The essence of this idea is encapsulated in a timeless Chinese proverb: "If you want to be happy for an hour, then take a nap. If you want to be happy for a day, then go for a picnic. If you want to be happy for a month, then get married. If you want to be happy for a year, then inherit a fortune. But if you want to be happy all your life, then go ahead and help others."

This may seem idealistic to some, but in contemporary times, even large corporations are recognising the importance of focusing on stakeholders beyond mere shareholder value. Take, for instance, the Tata Group—a conglomerate that views its community not just as shareholders but as integral contributors to its success. The group's unique model involves a significant portion of its profits being held by a trust dedicated to serving the community through healthcare, education, research institutions, and various social causes.

This approach extends beyond corporations, with many others embracing the shift towards Corporate Social Responsibility (CSR). Corporates allocate funds, as per norms, to CSR initiatives aimed at the betterment of the community. These funds are directed towards providing free education, shelter, medical facilities, and more to the underprivileged. This shift signifies a broader understanding of a mission or goal in life—one that goes beyond personal success and extends into serving the community.

Embracing this attitude prompts a crucial question: "How is our work contributing to the greater good and serving a larger purpose that benefits the community?"

"The surest way to happiness is to lose yourself in a cause greater than yourself."

—**Unknown**

"WHAT IS THE PUZZLE TO BE SOLVED?"

In the pursuit of our life's mission, it's common for people to be discouraged when faced with obstacles and challenges. The key, however, lies in changing our perspective and treating these challenges not as roadblocks, but as puzzles waiting to be solved. This shift in mindset transforms obstacles into opportunities, infusing us with renewed energy and motivation.

Solving puzzles requires creativity and often collaboration. Complex challenges are better addressed by seeking inputs from various sources and being open to asking for help. Embracing feedback, even if critical, is a powerful tool for growth. Rather than viewing criticism negatively, see it as a valuable opportunity to learn, adapt and improve.

Prepare yourself to embrace feedback and face criticism without hesitation or guilt. Remember, mistakes are an integral part of being human; accepting them is a mark of humility.

Break your day into small, achievable tasks that challenge you to do better each time. Eliminate distractions, concentrate on your skills and commit to continuous improvement.

In the intricate tapestry of life, challenges and problems are inevitable; suffering due to them is, however, optional. It is crucial to grasp the wisdom in John Milton's *Paradise Lost*, where Satan observes, "The mind is its own place, and in itself can make a Heaven of Hell, a Hell of Heaven." My father used to often quote William Shakespeare's insight in *Hamlet*: "There is nothing either good or bad, but thinking makes it so." These timeless quotes underscore the transformative power of our perception. Problems become opportunities for growth when viewed through a positive lens. By aligning our thoughts with this perspective, we not only navigate challenges with resilience but also unlock our creative potential, evolving into empowered individuals both personally and professionally.

By adopting this approach, you will not only progress towards your goals, but also attain a level of world-class excellence. Stay committed to the journey, solve the puzzles that come your way, and watch as your purpose unfolds into a meaningful, impactful life.

> **"Count your age by friends, not years. Count your life by smiles, not tears."**
>
> **—John Lennon**

THE STORY THAT WE TELL OURSELVES

In our relentless pursuit of discovering life's purpose, passion emerges as the compass, navigating us through the intricate maze of choices. To unearth our moments of flow, we require a narrative – an intricate story that eloquently narrates why we embark on this journey and the conscientious efforts invested in reaching our goals. Ashwath Damodaran, the esteemed

Professor of Finance at the Stern School of Business at New York University, illuminates the transformative power of stories. Whether valuing a startup or evaluating our own worth, it transcends mere numerical calculations, delving into the realms of purpose, ideologies, and endeavours.

As we traverse the tapestry of life, the significance of clarity regarding our purpose cannot be overstated. Consistently questioning what we are learning, contributing, and how our endeavours resonate with society ensures that we remain aligned with the pursuit of our purpose. The profound wisdom of Mother Teresa resonates, urging us to be mindful that every interaction leaves others better and happier.

In this introspective journey, seeking perfection and aspiring to attain world-class excellence becomes the driving force behind our endeavours. Life, when viewed as an adventure, encourages us to craft a narrative – a story filled with passion, purpose, and positive contributions to the world. When introducing ourselves to the world, contemplating the story we wish to tell becomes imperative. Gradually, as we engage in the process of writing and creating this narrative, our passion and purpose begin to unfold, weaving a compelling tale that not only inspires us but also brings pride to our loved ones.

The stories we weave for ourselves hold unparalleled significance as they serve as the nucleus of our lives, shaping our decisions and influencing the course of our journey. In Clayton Christensen's insightful book, *How Will You Measure Your Life?*, a compelling example underscores the transformative power of stories. Before the publication of *The Innovator's Dilemma*, Christensen received a call from Andrew Grove, Intel's chairman at the time. Grove, intrigued by Christensen's early papers on disruptive technology, sought his insights for Intel. In response, rather than providing directives, Clayton chose to narrate the story of Nucor steel—a tale illustrating how disruptive innovation permeated an industry as robust as steel. Through this story, Clayton didn't just dictate conclusions; he imparted a valuable skill—the ability to think critically. By guiding Grove through the narrative, Clayton empowered him to reach informed decisions independently. This narrative approach, highlighting the power of stories, becomes a potent tool in shaping our own lives.

A PASSIONATE PURSUIT OF THE GOAL, BUT INDIFFERENT TO OUTCOMES

Embracing the concept of being passionately dedicated to the pursuit of a goal while maintaining indifference to its outcomes is indeed a challenging paradox. This idea is deeply ingrained in various spiritual teachings, with the Bhagavad Gita, for instance, emphasising the importance of detaching from results. The notion is beautifully captured in the phrase "Man proposes, God disposes", suggesting that while humans can set goals, the ultimate outcome lies beyond their control. Philosophically, our lives are akin to a grand theatrical production, as Shakespeare eloquently noted, where we play our roles and navigate the unfolding scenes.

Before the culmination of a goal, enthusiasm and meticulous planning are crucial. As Aristotle aptly put it, happiness is the settling of the soul into its most appropriate spot. Planning becomes the first creation – envisioning the goal, contemplating the necessary investments, and assembling the required team. For instance, if one aspires to reach the moon, meticulous planning involving the required investment and personnel is indispensable. Clear milestones must be identified to navigate the journey effectively.

While passionate planning is essential, once the goal is attained, or even if the outcome diverges from expectations, cultivating a sense of indifference becomes imperative. This mindset is rooted in the understanding that the journey itself is an adventure. Just like the excitement and planning leading to the summit, indifference toward the outcome ensures a sustained sense of happiness. It encapsulates the wisdom that, in the grand play of life, our roles may be predestined, but our approach and attitude remain within our control.

> **"The happiness of your life depends upon the quality of your thoughts."**
>
> **—Marcus Aurelius**

RISK-TAKING

Bob had big dreams of running a marathon. Every day, he'd wake up, look at his "Future Marathoner" poster and promptly sit on the couch, eating chips while watching fitness videos. Months passed and Bob hadn't run a single step.

When a friend asked why, Bob said, "I'm waiting for the perfect weather." Eventually, Bob realised his real hurdle wasn't the weather—it was himself. Like Bob, many individuals, despite having a clear goal and vision, find themselves reluctant to take the first step into the unknown. This hesitation, depicted as being institutionalised, stems from mental constraints, social pressures, and a lack of confidence. The phrase "Don't rest on your laurels" echoes the notion that constraints are often products of our imagination. Like a frog in a well, conditioned to believe it is the entire world, individuals remain trapped in their perceived limitations.

The essence of taking risks in life lies in breaking free from the mental constraints that often bind us, akin to the story of the conditioned elephant or the crabs in a box. Over time, our initial resistance to limitations becomes acceptance, leading us to believe in a confined destiny. The movie "The Shawshank Redemption" beautifully captures this dilemma, highlighting the tendency to remain institutionalised in comfort zones.

Yet, human potential knows no bounds, and achievements are constrained only by the limitations we impose on ourselves.

Taking risks is not about abandoning all caution; rather, it requires a well-thought-out risk management strategy. Entrepreneurs often advise taking risks earlier in life, before commitments grow exponentially. Acknowledging that risks and fears may materialise, it becomes essential to develop a strategic approach. A prudent method is to explore one's passion gradually, perhaps starting on weekends while maintaining a stable job. This approach allows for an assessment of whether the newfound passion aligns with one's capabilities and is, indeed, the right calling.

The risk management strategy involves careful evaluation, as illustrated by the founders of Warby Parker. They did not immediately quit their jobs after college, but continued working on their startup alongside their weekday commitments. This incremental approach allowed them to gauge the business's viability before taking the plunge full-time. Such thoughtful risk management minimises the potential negative impact on personal and family life while pursuing newfound passions.

> **"Happiness resides not in possessions and not in gold; happiness dwells in the soul."**
>
> **—Democritus**

GOAL-SETTING

Once we've identified our life's purpose, the next crucial step is to set an audacious goal that sparks inspiration and motivates us to wake up with zeal each morning. Contrary to the traditional SMART goal-setting approach—specific, measurable, achievable, realistic, and time-bound—I argue that audacious goals, those that induce a bit of fear and seem unrealistic, are more likely to ignite our passion and drive. These goals should extend beyond mere selfish aspirations and carry the potential to bring substantial positive change to the community and society.

JRD Tata wisely noted that the community is not just another stakeholder but the very purpose of an enterprise's existence. Similarly, as individuals, our presence in this world should transcend mere self-interests. Rather than merely participating in the race, we should aspire to be the sole contender, leaving a lasting impact on the world, akin to companies like Xerox, Google, Walmart, or Apple, which have set benchmarks in their respective domains.

Setting an audacious goal serves as a personal challenge, encouraging us to think beyond our perceived limitations. The sheer magnitude of such a goal pushes our minds to consider innovative and unconventional ways to achieve it. Moreover, the universe tends to conspire in our favour when we commit to such audacious pursuits, providing unexpected avenues and opportunities.

Breaking down the audacious goal into manageable milestones is essential, and I recommend limiting audacious goals to 3 or 4 per year. This ensures balance, including spiritual goals, as we pursue multiple aspects of personal growth. However, the privacy of these goals is paramount. External opinions, even from close confidantes and well-wishers, can inadvertently discourage us. Goal-setting is a personal exercise, and the passion and energy to achieve the goal should be intrinsic.

To effectively work towards audacious goals, meticulous prioritisation of daily activities is necessary. Scheduling dedicated time for contemplation, research, and brainstorming, even if the path is not immediately clear, is crucial. By making consistent daily improvements of 1%, compounded over time, we inch closer to becoming 36 times better in a year's time.

Faith is a driving force in achieving audacious goals. Committing wholeheartedly and developing confidence in our abilities, even when the path may not be apparent, is imperative. Confidence and competence are interlinked; as we become more competent, our confidence grows. Building a support system comprising mentors, coaches, and like-minded friends further reinforces our faith and competence.

Visualising the audacious goal daily, as if it has already been achieved, creates excitement and encouragement. This mental rehearsal, similar to how sportspeople visualise games before playing them, aligns our energies and focus, propelling us toward the audacious goal. In essence, setting audacious goals becomes the key to happiness, allowing us to channel our energy, focus, and passion into a state of flow.

*"You have to **dream** before your dreams can come true."*
—Dr. A.P.J. Abdul Kalam

CONCLUSION

Ever wondered if your work could be your source of joy? In this chapter, we explored the connection between your passion and profession, revealing that true fulfilment comes when you get paid for doing what you love.

KEY TAKEAWAYS

1. **Fusion of Passion and Profession:**   Find that sweet spot where your passion intersects with your profession. It's not just a job; it's a gratifying journey when these 2 align.

2. **Purpose-Infused Tasks:**   Want to achieve flow? Your tasks need a bigger purpose. Learn from the stonecutter who wasn't just cutting stones; he was building a cathedral. Infuse purpose into your work.

3. **Leadership's Role:**   If you're a leader, ponder on this: Are you giving your team a sense of purpose? Your role is not just about tasks; it's about inspiring your team with a larger mission.

4. **Contribution Beyond Roles:**   Even without a leadership position, reflect on how your work serves a larger purpose. Understand the impact on the organisation and end users. That clarity rejuvenates your motivation.

5. **Continuous Clarity Pursuit:**   Keep asking: What's my mission? What's the organisation's mission? This ongoing exploration ensures sustained motivation and a clear direction.

> *"If you want to live a happy life,*
> *tie it to a goal, not to people or things."*
>
> —**Albert Einstein**

CHAPTER 2

THE ENDS DON'T JUSTIFY THE MEANS: DEVELOPING THE RIGHT ATTITUDE

INTRODUCTION:

In the last chapter, you embarked on the quest to find the purpose of your life. You've learned that even if the mission isn't immediately clear, the journey of seeking it is crucial. You've been encouraged to stay devoted to your current endeavours and to find micro flow events throughout the day, immersing yourself fully in each task. This approach is vital to prevent feeling overwhelmed.

Now, let's assume you've either discovered your life's mission or are in the process of doing so. This chapter is tailored for you, irrespective of where you are in your journey. It's about cultivating a set of attitudes or habits crucial for working towards your goals without losing perspective or compromising your happiness.

As various spiritual texts like the Bhagavad Gita have emphasised, happiness lies in the act of doing, not just in the results. True happiness springs from the journey, not merely the destination. This understanding is essential as you experience the flow in your tasks. It's not the end result that brings fulfilment, but the process itself.

In this chapter, you'll dive deeper into developing the right attitude towards your work and daily tasks. Remember, what you control is the present moment. By cultivating the right mindset, you can make the most of each moment. Each small success, each moment lived fully, builds a path towards a brighter future, drawing you ever closer to the aspirations you hold dear.

While 23 attitudes may seem like a lot, my intent is to offer you a toolkit of ideas to consider. Take your time to go through them, adopting what resonates with you and leaving what doesn't. It's not about leveraging all of them, but finding the ones that align with your goals. Even adopting one or 2 attitudes, if done well, can make a meaningful difference in your life. Feel free to choose what makes sense to you and let the rest go.

Let's journey together through this chapter as you learn to balance passion for your work with a mindset that values the process over the end result. This balance is key to living a life that's not just goal-oriented, but also rich in happiness and fulfilment.

"I'm choosing happiness over suffering. I know I am. I'm making space for the unknown future to fill up my life with yet-to-come surprises."

—Elizabeth Gilbert

ATTITUDE 1

Don't Worry

Bobby McFerrin's song, "Don't worry, be happy," resonates deeply, doesn't it? Remember the lines, "In every life, we have some troubles. When you worry, you make it double; So don't worry, be happy"? It's more than just a melody; it's a life lesson. You, like many others, might often find yourself caught up in worrying about the future or lamenting the past. This habit, especially prevalent among those passionately working towards a mission, is a trap you should strive to avoid.

Worry brings negativity, cutting down what you could achieve in half. It fills your day with pressure and stress, leading to underperformance. The mind, a powerful tool, can sometimes paint unrealistic pictures, leading to a skewed perception of reality. If you constantly indulge in negative thoughts, you risk torturing yourself with a distorted view of the world.

So, ask yourself, "Is there any challenge in my life?" If the answer is yes, take a proactive approach. Write it down, seek help, try to solve it. Take action rather than just lamenting about the situation. Train your mind to focus on positivity and ways to overcome challenges. Every cloud has a silver lining; it's your job to find it and craft a strategy to address the problem.

Ignorance is often the biggest problem. Not knowing how to deal with a challenge can be paralysing. So, seek knowledge. Reach out to a coach or a mentor. Shift your perspective and tackle the problem from a different angle. Don't let worry consume and destroy you. Instead, let it be a catalyst for seeking solutions, gaining knowledge, and taking decisive action. Remember, worry doubles trouble, while action can halve it. Your mission is too important to be derailed by unwarranted worries.

> *"Don't waste your time in anger, regrets, worries, and grudges. Life is too short to be unhappy."*
> —**Roy T. Bennett**

ATTITUDE 2

Be Optimistic and Stay Positive

After exploring the importance of not worrying, let's delve into the essence of optimism and positivity. A simple yet powerful way to maintain a positive outlook is to find reasons to laugh. Have you noticed how often people get overly serious in conversations, their body language reeking of stress? Lighten up a bit; laughter can be incredibly therapeutic.

Acting positively isn't just a temporary facade; over time, it becomes a part of who you are. Embrace a life strategy focused on recognising and appreciating your blessings. Be grateful for the opportunities you have to serve others, and this gratitude will propel you towards achieving your mission. Often, people dwell on the negatives because they lack the fortitude to acknowledge and appreciate the positives in their lives. This outlook can also lead to forgetting to thank those who have helped along the way. Changing this attitude is crucial.

Consider the classic example of the glass: instead of viewing it as half empty, choose to see it as half full. It's a matter of perspective, shifting focus from what's missing to what's present. Regularly remind yourself of your fortunes. Reflect on the privileges you have, like ample food, a home, quality education, and other essentials. Comparing your situation to those less fortunate can deepen your appreciation for what you have.

A practical method to sustain this positive outlook is to maintain a gratitude journal. Make it a daily practice to jot down the positive aspects of your life and reflect on them. This habit not only fosters positivity, but also enhances mindfulness and contentment.

Don't forget the power of expressing gratitude. Take the time to send messages, emails, or voice notes to thank people for their support. Expressing gratitude consistently not only puts you in a positive frame of mind, but also boosts your creativity and optimism. It's a virtuous cycle; the more gratitude you express, the more positive and optimistic you become, enhancing your ability to face challenges and pursue your goals with renewed vigour.

A Note of Caution: Sincere Gratitude

As you embrace the practice of expressing gratitude, remember it must be both sincere and perceived as such. Reflect on a story shared by Andrew Carnegie in his book where he highlights the essence of genuine appreciation. Carnegie's anecdote reveals that gratitude should be altruistic and unconditional, not motivated by personal gain. The true power of gratitude lies in its ability to empower others by recognising their contributions sincerely.

However, sometimes there's a hesitation, a fear of how your appreciation might be perceived. This apprehension can stem from a concern about appearing disingenuous or having ulterior motives. Overcome this fear. It's crucial to not let these worries hold you back from offering sincere praise. The reality is, the vast majority of people can distinguish between genuine appreciation and flattery. They know how to accept a heartfelt compliment.

Therefore, as you continue on your journey of gratitude, remember that your expressions of thanks should come from a place of authenticity. Your aim is not to impress, but to genuinely acknowledge and appreciate the efforts of others. Such sincerity not only uplifts the recipients but also enriches your own sense of well-being and connectedness. In doing so, you contribute to a culture of genuine appreciation and positivity, one that can profoundly impact both personal and professional relationships. Remember, true appreciation is a gift that keeps on giving, fostering an environment of mutual respect and gratitude.

ATTITUDE 3

Live in an Unhurried Way

In the hustle of life, it's common to find yourself juggling numerous activities, feeling lost and overwhelmed. While it's fine to focus on multiple tasks, the key is to avoid doing too many things at once. Remember our discussion on achieving flow from the last chapter? It's just as important to concentrate solely on those tasks that are crucial at the moment. Prioritisation is vital here; try not to overload yourself with simultaneous activities.

There's an insightful saying: "Sometimes to go fast, we need to go slow." This paradoxical wisdom holds true in many aspects of life, especially when striving for efficiency and effectiveness in your work. By slowing down, you can start to relish your tasks, appreciate the present moment, and enhance your performance. When you slow down, you give yourself the opportunity to do each task better, to bring in your creativity, and to truly enjoy what you're doing.

Living in an unhurried way doesn't mean being less productive. On the contrary, it allows you to be present in the moment, giving your full attention and best effort to the task at hand. This approach leads to higher quality work, greater satisfaction and a deeper sense of fulfilment.

So, as you go about your daily tasks, remember to take a step back, breathe, and focus. Give yourself permission to slow down. This will not only improve your productivity and creativity, but also enhance your overall well-being. Living unhurriedly is about finding balance, allowing yourself to be fully engaged in the present, and savouring the richness of each moment.

> *"The truly wise and happy are never rushed."*
>
> —**Maxime Lagacé**

ATTITUDE 4

Developing Good Habits

To foster happiness in your life, it's essential to establish and maintain good habits within your daily routine. These habits serve as foundational blocks for a fulfilling and balanced life. Start by ensuring that you incorporate some form of exercise into your day. Physical activity not only keeps your body healthy, but also energises your mind, preparing you for the challenges ahead.

Equally important is setting aside time for contemplation and prayer. These moments of introspection and spiritual connection provide mental peace and clarity, which are crucial in today's fast-paced world. They allow you to centre yourself and approach your tasks with a calm and focused mind.

Don't overlook the significance of making time for family, friends, and nurturing relationships. These interactions are vital for emotional well-being and provide a sense of belonging and support. When these good habits are ingrained in your daily life and practiced with discipline, they collectively contribute to a reservoir of energy and positivity, fuelling your other scheduled tasks throughout the day.

I've observed many people who are so intensely focused on their goals that they tend to neglect the simpler yet crucial aspects of life like health, relationships, and spiritual well-being. They pack their schedules with back-to-back meetings, giving themselves no time to rest or recharge. In the long run, this approach can take a toll on their health and overall effectiveness, and their capacity to give their best in any task diminishes.

Therefore, as you continue to pursue your goals, remember the importance of these fundamental habits. Balancing your aspirations with self-care, relationships, and spiritual practices ensures not only the achievement of your goals, but also the maintenance of your overall health and happiness. Developing and adhering to these good habits is not just about discipline; it's about creating a lifestyle that supports and enhances your journey towards success and fulfilment.

ATTITUDE 5

Practising Negative Visualisation

I once heard someone say, "The worst thing that can happen is showing up at work in your pyjamas," which seemed ridiculous—until I actually did it. Yes, in the early days of remote work, I confidently strolled into a video meeting, completely forgetting that I hadn't switched from home mode to work mode. Turns out, everyone had a good laugh, and after that day, I was mentally prepared for just about anything—including double-checking the camera angle.

Now, as funny as that moment was, it taught me the value of asking, "What's the worst that can happen?"

This question is very liberating because it truly questions the negative thoughts in our minds in a particular situation. By asking ourselves this question, we prepare our minds for the worst possible situation. Once we identify that, we can start planning and working on that situation so that we can be mentally prepared and handle it in a creative and balanced fashion.

It is said that world-class basketball players and other sportsmen rehearse their game many times before actually playing, so that they can be mentally prepared and can handle any kind of situation.

That is what this question or negative visualisation does, by preparing a person to be ready for the worst.

It challenges your mind to be prepared for the worst possible scenario. You are continuously simulating how to react to it so you don't break down under extreme pressure and stressful situations. It is a very good practice that happy people adopt for reacting positively in a negative situation and keeping their temperament positive.

ATTITUDE 6

Focusing on the Important Rather Than on the Urgent

Many times in our daily schedule, we spend focusing on the tasks which are urgent, putting out fires, and hardly leave any time for what is truly important. Hence, it is imperative and a prerogative to classify the tasks according to priority. Plan our day in a detailed manner and list down the tasks in categories of important and also urgent. This will keep us well informed and make our day meaningful.

Listing down will help in sorting the tasks according to the priority, and it will also ensure that all our important tasks are completed properly, and the non-important things are kept aside.

It is often said that if we choose to improve ourselves by 1% every day, then by the end of the year, or 365 days, we will be 36 times better off than when we started.

It is necessary to be organised and systematic in life, and by focusing on the truly important things, we can exponentially improve ourselves.

ATTITUDE 7

Dedicated Focus on the Things That One Can Control

Many times, I have seen that whenever there is a stressful situation, people start talking about it and discussing how it is so much out of control. This is a practice that derails happiness not only of the responsible person who has been assigned the task but also of the entire team when he starts discussing completely out-of-control activities or tasks.

Hence, whether you are a leader or some personnel trying to gain better control of the situation, you should have the habit of asking yourself a very important question: "What is in our control, and what is not in our control?"

Learn the habit of keeping aside the things that are not in control, rather than continuously worrying about them. I have seen that people who focus on the things that are in their control start making improvements. They are continuously expanding their circle of influence and are then able to address the things that are on the edges of their control, and gradually work towards controlling things that are totally out of control.

A good example is, you know, if we are working in a team, there are many things that an individual or a team is dependent on: another person or other team members to do.

That situation can be considered out of control. So, rather than complaining that the other people are not pulling in their way, it is better to focus on the task that one is doing and is responsible for. And do it so well that it inspires the team to all start putting in quality efforts and get respect from the other team.

Eventually, I have also seen in my personal life that it truly starts inspiring the other team members. They also start pulling themselves up in match to the perfection of the task that one is accomplishing.

The main point is not to start complaining about why others are not putting in the effort; rather, it is better to start giving your best to what needs to be done and do it at your level best.

And not keep worrying about the things that are not in our control.

ATTITUDE 8

Appreciate Imperfection

Indeed, one of the qualities that truly happy people possess is their ability to appreciate imperfection in themselves, others, and the world around them. Life is inherently imperfect; situations can be messy, and people are flawed, including ourselves. It's crucial to acknowledge this truth and let go of the unrealistic expectation that everything should be perfect.

Consider this: if we ourselves are not perfect, why should we expect perfection from others? This unreasonable demand for perfection is often a significant source of our unhappiness. Instead, we can adopt a simple yet powerful attitude: appreciation of imperfection. Start by asking yourself, "How can I contribute to making things better?"

Let's draw inspiration from Mahatma Gandhi's story. When he returned from South Africa to attend a meeting of the Indian National Congress, he encountered a dirty lavatory.

Instead of complaining or waiting for someone else to clean it, he took action. Gandhi grabbed a bucket of water and began cleaning the urinal himself. He didn't do it to impress others; he did it for his own satisfaction. The other delegates were shocked, but Gandhi's acceptance of imperfection drove him to find a solution rather than dwell on the problem.

This is the kind of attitude we should cultivate in our lives. We must recognise that situations won't always be perfect, but the crucial question is, "What are we going to do about it?" Even when we can't change the circumstances, we can choose to accept them and find beauty in their imperfections. By appreciating imperfection, we can live more contented and meaningful lives.

Another way to appreciate imperfection is to inculcate humour. Especially, laughing at yourself for imperfect execution or a situation is a good attitude that keeps you in a positive state of mind. I see this consistently among top leaders who have the maturity to laugh at themselves. This not only lightens up the situation but also makes them real and much more authentic. Incorporating this attitude in your own life can help you embrace imperfections with grace and authenticity.

> **"Happiness is when what you think, what you say, and what you do are in harmony."**
> —**Mahatma Gandhi**

ATTITUDE 9

Redefining Success and Failure

It's essential to develop a unique perspective on success and failure, one that doesn't conform to traditional norms. Often, we tend to view success and failure through the wrong lens, measuring them against external benchmarks. This mindset can lead to negativity and dissatisfaction. To foster lasting happiness, adopt an attitude that acknowledges you are already successful.

Consider your own body, a marvel of biology and intricate coordination among countless cells and processes. Acknowledge the sheer wonder of your body's functionality. Many people around the world suffer from illnesses that prevent them from leading normal lives. Thus, simply having a healthy, functional body can be seen as a form of success.

In the realm of work, it's common for managers to set goals and targets as motivational tools. However, when these targets are set unrealistically high, they can demotivate employees. Instead, goals should be practical, measurable, achievable, and aspirational. This balanced approach generates the necessary momentum without overwhelming individuals.

Furthermore, it's crucial to celebrate even small successes. Large organisations often overlook this practice, focusing too much on high profitability and ignoring innovations serving the lower end of the market. Embracing the habit of celebrating small victories not only propels personal growth but also creates a supportive environment for friends, peers, and family members. By appreciating small achievements, we foster motivation to achieve more significant milestones in life.

ATTITUDE 10

What is the Learning Opportunity Here?

Instead of viewing success and failure as mere milestones, we should shift our perspective and ask a different question: "What can I learn from this experience?" When we adopt this mindset and treat every challenge as a puzzle to be solved, we cultivate a habit of welcoming challenges rather than avoiding them.

In life, we often develop preferences and aversions. Unfortunately, we tend to dislike challenges or changes in our routines. To foster lasting happiness, we must learn to embrace challenges with open arms and avoid despising them. It's crucial to understand that situations won't always unfold as we expect, and that's perfectly normal.

Instead of feeling discouraged by failures, we should view them as opportunities for growth. Embrace challenges and ask yourself, "What can I learn from this situation?" Remember the age-old saying, "What doesn't kill you, makes you stronger." Rather than berating yourself for not meeting certain benchmarks, consider each difficulty as a valuable chance to improve and grow.

By adopting this attitude, you'll experience more moments of happiness and be less discouraged when facing the first signs of adversity. Embracing challenges and seeking opportunities for learning will become second nature, leading to a happier, and more fulfilling life.

> *"The greater part of our happiness or misery depends upon our dispositions, and not upon our circumstances."*
> —Martha Washington

ATTITUDE 11

Lifelong Learner

When we observe successful individuals, it often stirs 2 contrasting emotions within us. On one hand, we admire their accomplishments and expertise, while on the other hand, we may feel a twinge of envy or misery seeing them so content and accomplished. The most constructive attitude in such moments is to appreciate these individuals and ask ourselves, "What can I learn from this person?"

By identifying the positive qualities and actions that have contributed to their success, we can endeavour to incorporate similar traits into our own lives. According to Robert Stenberg, the President of "Vu Intelligence," purposeful engagement is the key to achieving expertise. This means that when we focus our attention and effort on a particular task for a significant amount of time, such as roughly 10,000 hours (equivalent to about 10 years of life), we inevitably become highly skilled in that area.

In fact, with dedicated practice, we can become among the best in the world at what we do. Furthermore, scientific research has revealed that the human brain has the capacity to learn throughout our entire lives, and it continues to develop as we age. Surprisingly, we typically use only 10% of our brain's true potential.

Therefore, we should view life as an ongoing opportunity for learning and growth. Instead of striving solely to prove our worth to others, we should actively seek ways to learn, gain new experiences and enhance our personal development. While it's essential to steer clear of destructive criticism from peers and friends, we should invite constructive self-critique that fosters our self-esteem and encourages personal growth.

In this pursuit, we should also focus on developing skills and knowledge in areas where we may currently lack expertise. Lifelong learning is a fundamental attitude that can significantly contribute to our happiness and well-being. It's an attitude worth cultivating and embracing throughout our lives.

ATTITUDE 12

Taking Responsibility

It's not uncommon to encounter people who have a tendency to blame the world, circumstances, or others for their failures or shortcomings. At times, this might even feel like an enticing path to follow, and placing blame on external factors can provide momentary relief. However, I'd like you to contemplate a question: "Are we truly living in a world where everyone and everything is conspiring against us?" The honest answer is no.

Embracing such an attitude of blaming the world not only hinders our own happiness but also negatively impacts our relationships with others. It's essential to remind ourselves that the world is, in fact, a marvellous place to live. As Shakespeare eloquently put it, "There is nothing good or bad in this world, but thinking makes it so."

Instead of blaming others, we should practice forgiveness for small mistakes and understand that people's behaviour is influenced by the values they hold, which may not always align with our own. Developing empathy and acceptance is crucial in these situations.

Furthermore, it's important to acknowledge that the consequences we face are often a direct result of our own actions and decisions. Rather than shifting blame comfortably onto someone or something else, we should question why we find ourselves in a particular situation and identify the underlying causes.

Once we accept responsibility for our circumstances, we can then focus on making improvements. Much like the example of Mahatma Gandhi, who encountered a dirty public toilet and took it upon himself to clean it, we must take ownership of our situation and actively seek ways to make it better.

While we may not reach the level of greatness exemplified by Mahatma Gandhi, we should nonetheless commit to taking responsibility for our lives and striving to enhance our current situations. It is in this journey of self-accountability that we can find a path to happiness and personal growth.

"You are responsible for your life. You can't keep blaming somebody else for your dysfunction. Life is really about moving on."

—Oprah Winfrey

ATTITUDE 13

Nothing Gets Done Without Hard Work

I once worked with someone who had a unique approach to deadlines. They'd always say, "I don't procrastinate. I just wait until the last minute because I thrive under pressure." One day, with a looming deadline just hours away, I asked how their progress was going. With a completely straight face, they replied, "Oh, I've done all the important work…mentally."

Needless to say, the rest of us were burning the midnight oil to hit that deadline! It's a reminder that while creativity is great, success comes from rolling up your sleeves and getting things done—mentally and physically.

I've encountered 2 types of people in my life: those who shy away from hard work and spend their time complaining about it, accomplishing little, and those who roll up their sleeves and diligently tackle their tasks without a hint of complaint.

It's crucial to realise that success is not handed to us on a silver platter. It doesn't come effortlessly; we must be willing to put in the effort and burn the midnight oil to reach our goals. This attitude of embracing hard work brings us closer to our objectives.

We should learn to accept that challenges are presented to us because we possess the capability to overcome them. Instead of wasting time complaining or evading challenges, we should wholeheartedly accept them and conquer them head-on.

I often come across individuals who live in a state of constant denial, claiming that challenges are beyond their control. However, this narrative is far from the truth. Most of the time, challenges are within our control if we make the effort to understand and address them.

Let me share a thought-provoking story to illustrate this point. Imagine finding yourself in the middle of a desert, utterly disoriented with no sense of direction. You don't know where you are, and there are no visible landmarks in sight. The question you must ask yourself is, "What should I do?"

Would you sit in the desert and passively wait for help, or would you randomly choose a direction and start walking? The answer is clear: you would pick a direction and begin moving. By taking action, you increase your chances of success from 0% to 25%. Even if you end up going in the wrong direction, you're closer to your goal than if you had remained still.

Sitting idly in the desert might lead to sunstroke and peril, but by making an effort to find the right direction, you enhance your chances of success. It's imperative to start working hard, as hard work indeed pays off. You may not find the solution immediately, but you will eventually discover the way forward.

Consider the example of Thomas Edison, who was once asked about his numerous attempts at inventing the light bulb. He replied, "To find success, I had to take a thousand steps. I didn't see those steps as failures, but rather as stepping stones to success." It's precisely this attitude we must cultivate to achieve both success and happiness.

ATTITUDE 14

Stop Judging

There are moments when our commitment to completing tasks leads us to become excessively critical, not just of ourselves, but also of those around us. This is an attitude that we need to steer clear of. As Mignon McLaughlin wisely said, "Nobody is perfect, and nobody deserves to be perfect. Nobody has it easy; everybody has issues. You never know what people are going through. So, pause before you start judging, criticising, or mocking others. Everybody is fighting their unique war."

It's essential to be transparently aware of our imperfections and be open to discussing them with the world. Unless we acknowledge our deficiencies and reach out for help when needed, how can we ever hope to improve?

By continuously convincing ourselves that we are perfect in areas where we are not, we deceive ourselves in the short run but ultimately suffer in the long run. Neither the world nor we are perfect, but we are fortunate to have been given the unique opportunity to learn and grow every day. Each day is a gift, offering us the chance to enhance ourselves and refine our craft.

At the end of the day, success is about stretching our abilities and working smarter. Intelligence and fame are attributes people achieve through concerted effort. Take, for example, Michael Jordan, a basketball legend. His tremendous success and the admiration he received from people were the results of relentless practice and hard work. His coach once said, "Michael Jordan is a hard-working champion. He earned his name and fame through sheer determination. He was the first person to arrive at the court and the last person to leave."

The same holds true for other sports icons like Sachin Tendulkar. Their work ethic, dedication, and commitment are what made them famous. They acknowledged their weaknesses and tirelessly worked to overcome them. They never boasted about knowing everything, but instead, they kept putting in effort to motivate not only themselves but also their teams.

Even at the peak of their careers, they remained humble and continued to work harder. They weren't born with a silver spoon; their success and fame were the results of diligent effort and hard work. This is an attitude we should strive to develop as well.

"There is no happiness like that of being loved by your fellow creatures, and feeling that your presence is an addition to their comfort."

—**Charlotte Brontë**

ATTITUDE 15

Doing Whatever it Takes

Another quality that happy individuals possess, and an essential attitude to cultivate, revolves around how we respond to setbacks. The way we handle setbacks can determine our happiness and success. So ask yourself, "Do setbacks make me more determined to succeed, or do they lead me towards depression and self-doubt? Do they make me feel incompetent, or do they ignite a renewed sense of energy, pushing me to tackle challenges more creatively?"

As the age-old saying goes, "Winners don't quit, and quitters don't win." To find happiness, we must adopt a mindset that doesn't fear failure. Failure is merely a stepping stone on our path, and it should never define our capabilities or self-worth. We must consistently remind ourselves that we can achieve success.

To unleash our full potential, we need to put in an extraordinary amount of effort, often 10 times more than we initially imagine. This effort is what transforms our potential into tangible accomplishments. It has the power to reshape us as individuals, driving us to new heights.

In the movie *The Pursuit of Happiness*, Will Smith imparts the same wisdom to his son when the boy contemplates giving up on playing basketball. He tells him, "Don't let anyone tell you that you can't do something. If you have a dream, you need to protect it. People who can't do something themselves will tell you that you can't do it. If you want something, go get it, period. If you want something from the core of your heart, then you need to develop the habit of not giving up. Do whatever it takes to achieve your goal and put in efforts, not just 1x or 2x, but 10x the effort to achieve it."

If you've taken the time to discover what you love in the first chapter and have found your Ikigai, then you'll be engaged in activities you genuinely enjoy. When you continuously learn and take pleasure in what you love to do, you'll have the right attitude to sustain your journey towards your goals. This is crucial for achieving happiness and success in life.

> *"Everyone wants to live on top of the mountain, but all the happiness and growth occurs while you're climbing it."*
> —Andy Rooney

ATTITUDE 16

Play the Game That You Can Win

Let me draw an analogy to emphasise a critical point. People often enjoy playing games in casinos. Initially, they may experience some wins, which elicit euphoria and entice them to continue playing. However, over time, they tend to lose more than they gain, leading to disappointment. When you enter a casino, you must recognise one undeniable fact: in the long run, the casino always wins.

Similarly, in life, no matter how positive your attitude, if you choose a profession or pursue a path that is virtually impossible to succeed in, you'll find yourself unhappy. It's akin to repeatedly forcing yourself against an insurmountable wall or banging your head against it, which ultimately leads to unhappiness and, in some cases, depression.

If you're working in an environment where appreciation and positive outcomes are scarce, sustaining motivation can be incredibly challenging. Therefore, my recommendation is to be exceptionally cautious when choosing the "game" you want to play – a career, a path, or a pursuit.

Consider the example of the legendary athlete, Michael Jordan. When he tragically lost his father, he was deeply affected and decided to temporarily step away from basketball to try his hand at playing baseball. Despite his incredible work ethic and dedication, he did not achieve the same level of success in baseball as he did in basketball. Why? Because he was not passionate about baseball; basketball was his true calling. Fortunately, he recognised this early on and returned to basketball, becoming one of the greatest athletes in history.

In our own lives, we must make similarly wise choices. We need to identify what we excel at and be realistic about our abilities. Every individual possesses something unique within them. The key is to discover that distinctive value we can offer to the world.

Perhaps you've watched the iconic Bollywood movie "3 Idiots" where Aamir Khan's character imparts a valuable lesson to his friends. He tells them, "Lata Mangeshkar would not be the singing queen if she had decided to become a cricketer, and Sachin Tendulkar would not be a famous cricketer if he had tried his hand at singing." His message encourages his friends to follow their hearts, pursue the work they love, and excel in it. As they heed his advice, they transform from losers to winners. This illustrates the essence of playing a game that you can win.

This journey begins with humility, as we honestly assess ourselves and work on cultivating our unique abilities that can bring value to the world.

While it's essential to play to our strengths, it's equally important to acknowledge and address key weaknesses. Ignoring critical areas that require attention can hinder progress and lead to dissatisfaction. However, the right attitude lies in understanding where our true strengths lie and focusing our energy there. As Warren Buffet wisely says, "Play within your circle of competence." Knowing your core abilities, while managing key weaknesses, ensures a balanced approach to growth and happiness.

ATTITUDE 17

Develop a Strong Foundation

I'd like to share a remarkable story, illustrated beautifully by Robin Sharma, that underscores the importance of developing a strong foundation in life, much like the renowned painter, Picasso. In this story, a lady approached Picasso and made a simple request, "Picasso, could you create a small caricature of me?" Without hesitation, he agreed and, in a mere 5 minutes, crafted a lifelike portrait of her. However, when he handed it to her, Picasso declared, "My lady, that will be one million dollars."

Naturally, the lady was taken aback and questioned the seemingly exorbitant price for just a five-minute sketch. To this, Picasso replied with profound wisdom, "For you, it may appear to be only 5 minutes, but it took me 10 years to prepare and hone my skills to create this piece in just 5 minutes."

This anecdote serves as a poignant reminder that, like Picasso, we must consistently invest in our craft and lay a strong foundation. Regrettably, the significance of building a robust foundation is often overlooked.

While it is true that individuals with financial means can establish extensive networks and may have a higher likelihood of success, I want to underscore the paramount importance of a good education. Quality education serves as a Launchpad that propels us forward, significantly shortening the journey that many others might take to reach similar heights.

Therefore, it is essential to identify the foundational elements that will guide us towards our goals. These elements may include education, expanding our network, relocating to a different place or region, cultivating new friendships with more motivating, supportive, committed, and influential individuals, forming a new team, aligning ourselves with like-minded peers, or securing the necessary capital.

Regardless of the specific elements chosen, we should not embark on this journey alone. Instead, we should work on building a sturdy foundation. This foundation will not only support our endeavours but also contribute to our overall happiness. Furthermore, the returns on our investment in a strong foundation are likely to be far more rewarding than launching into an endeavour without the necessary groundwork.

Just as Picasso highlighted that it took a decade of dedication and practice to create a five-minute masterpiece, we must contemplate what we can achieve in just five minutes that others might labour over for nearly ten years to accomplish with the same level of precision and effectiveness.

This insight leads us to the realisation that we should prioritise building a strong foundation for enduring success and lasting happiness.

ATTITUDE 18

Staying Objective

Maintaining objectivity is another crucial attitude that can greatly contribute to your happiness and success. Our brains are wired in a way that any perception of the external world must pass through the reptilian brain network, which controls our emotions, before reaching the neo-cortex responsible for critical thinking and rational contemplation. This wiring often makes it challenging to remain objective as our emotions can cloud our judgement.

To overcome this physiological drawback, it's essential to learn to control your emotions, especially when making important decisions. If you find yourself in an emotionally charged situation, it's best to avoid making significant choices until you've had time to cool off and regain your composure. Simply stepping outside for a moment, having a glass of water, or adjourning a meeting and returning later can help dissipate the intense emotions that might lead to rash or erroneous decisions.

For instance, consider the legendary tale of Arjuna from the Mahabharata. When faced with the prospect of battling his own relatives, mentors, friends, and loved ones on the opposing side of the battlefield, Arjuna became emotionally overwhelmed and decided to lay down his weapons. In response, Lord Krishna intervened, counselling Arjuna to maintain objectivity. Krishna reminded him that, despite the personal connections, his duty as a Kshatriya was to fight. Arjuna needed to focus on his duty objectively, putting aside the overwhelming emotions he felt for his family.

The lesson here is clear: we must cultivate an attitude of objectivity in our dealings with the world. Training our minds to remain calm and rational, even in the face of stress or emotional turbulence, ensures that we make sound decisions and stay on course to reach our goals.

By thinking objectively and not allowing our emotions to cloud our judgement, we increase our chances of achieving success and experiencing lasting happiness.

> *"Happiness is when what you think, what you say,*
> *and what you do are in harmony."*
> —**Mahatma Gandhi**

ATTITUDE 19

Giving Your Best Shot Always

Giving your best effort consistently is a remarkable attitude that can lead to both excellence and lasting happiness. When you approach every situation, task, and moment in your day with the commitment to do your absolute best, you redefine the meaning of success. It becomes less about the outcome and more about the process and the effort you put into it.

By consistently giving your best, you experience a deep sense of satisfaction and happiness, regardless of external criticism or challenges. You know that you've poured your heart and soul into your work, which serves as its reward. Criticism doesn't deter you; instead, it motivates you further because you're confident in the quality of your efforts.

This attitude of wholehearted dedication also helps you stay focused and avoid distractions. Dwelling excessively on the end goal, whether it's winning a gold medal in academics or achieving a specific target at work, can increase stress and anxiety. Instead, it's advisable to concentrate on the work you have for the day and to execute it with world-class excellence.

For instance, aspiring to win a gold medal in studies is a noble goal, but obsessively thinking about it without dedicating the necessary effort to your studies won't lead to success. To earn that gold medal, you must focus on the daily tasks, study diligently, and strive for excellence in each subject. By giving your best every day, your chances of reaching the goal, without undue stress or hindrance, greatly increase.

In my own journey of becoming a gold medallist, I was deeply inspired by my grandfather, who was a gold medallist in one of the toughest banking exams in the country. My grandmother often showed me his achievements from a young age, and I decided early on that I wanted to follow in his footsteps. With perseverance, I not only became a gold medallist in my engineering studies but also in my MBA, where I was the overall college topper and elective course topper in marketing. Studying at top universities in India made this accomplishment even more significant.

I'm thankful that while my goal was to become a gold medallist, I didn't fixate on the end result. Instead, I focused on this simple goal of giving my best every day. I am also grateful to my parents for not putting any undue pressure on me. They never once entered my room to ask what I was doing.

They understood that I was working passionately and always reminded me that while effort is in my control, the results are a function of that effort. This understanding served as both a reminder and a motivation for me to continue pursuing my goals with determination, one step at a time.

In the workplace, when you're assigned a goal or target, constantly fixating on the end result can prove to be counterproductive. Instead, immerse yourself in your daily tasks, tackle them with excellence and maintain your commitment to doing your best. High-quality work, driven by your dedication, will ultimately lead you to your target with confidence and motivation.

In conclusion, adopting the attitude of giving your best in every aspect of life can transform your journey and redefine your success. It shifts the focus from external outcomes to the satisfaction found in dedicated effort. This mindset enables you to stay motivated, maintain your focus and, ultimately, achieve your goals with world-class excellence.

ATTITUDE 20

Being Humble

Maintaining humility is another essential attitude for lifelong happiness. While self-confidence is admirable, excessive arrogance or overconfidence can alienate others and hinder collaboration. Such arrogance not only risks losing support but also blinds us to the realities of the situation at hand. Ego can sometimes prevent us from seeking solutions with the help of others.

In an ever-changing world, particularly with the disruptions caused by digital technology, it is crucial to be open to criticism, accept feedback and embrace change. Being humble enough to acknowledge our lack of expertise in a new environment and seeking assistance to acquire the necessary knowledge is a valuable trait.

Andrew Carnegie, a prominent industrialist and philanthropist, once expressed his desire for his epitaph to read, "Here lies a man who was wise enough to bring into his service men who knew more than he did." This epitomises the humility required to recognise and leverage the expertise of others.

Another remarkable example of humility can be found in Jack Welch, who served as the CEO of General Electric (GE). When Welch assumed leadership, he placed a strong emphasis on values and teamwork over individual brilliance. He encouraged leaders to share credit with their teams, fostering a culture of collaboration. Under his leadership, GE underwent a significant cultural transformation, growing from a $14 million company in 1980 to one with a market capitalisation of $490 billion. This transformation demonstrated the power of humility and teamwork in achieving success.

A shining example from the world of entertainment is Bollywood superstar Amitabh Bachchan. Despite his immense fame, Bachchan faced financial difficulties when his company, ABCL Corporation, failed in the 1990s, leaving him in significant debt. His humility shone through as he approached directors he had previously worked with, sharing his problems and seeking their support. Bachchan's television show, "Kaun Banega Crorepati" (KBC), became a massive success. In a few years, he not only cleared his debts but also became even more prosperous and successful. His story illustrates how humility can endear a person to millions and lead to remarkable achievements.

In conclusion, cultivating humility is essential for lifelong happiness. It allows us to recognise the value of collaboration, seek help when needed and embrace change. By remaining humble, we can build strong relationships, inspire others and achieve remarkable success while staying grounded and connected with those around us.

> *"Happiness cannot be travelled to, owned, earned, worn, or consumed. Happiness is the spiritual experience of living every minute with love, grace, and gratitude."*
>
> —Denis Waitley

ATTITUDE 21

Stop Blaming and Start Doing

The attitude of not blaming others and instead taking responsibility for a situation is crucial for lifelong happiness and success. When we encounter challenging situations, it's essential to resist the urge to ascribe blame to external factors or individuals. Instead, we should ask ourselves, "What can we do now to address this situation and work toward a solution together?"

Consider a scenario where a boss faces a difficult situation and immediately shifts the blame onto their subordinates for their inability to perform or complete a task. While this may provide temporary satisfaction by deflecting responsibility, it ultimately undermines their leadership and erodes the support of their team. Blaming others not only avoids accountability, but also sets a negative tone, preventing the use of creative problem-solving skills to overcome challenges effectively.

In my own leadership experience, I encourage my team to take responsibility for their situations. I believe this empowers individuals to proactively seek solutions and work collaboratively with one another. Time and again, I've seen that we need to start acknowledging our role in the problems or challenges we face, no matter how small that role might be. This approach helps open doors to finding constructive ways to address issues. Such an attitude fosters a positive mindset, encourages teamwork and enables us to utilise our creative abilities to tackle even the most daunting tasks.

In summary, the attitude of refraining from blaming others and assuming responsibility for a situation is a fundamental aspect of happiness and success. It empowers us to face challenges head-on, collaborate effectively with others, and tap into our creativity to overcome obstacles and achieve our goals.

> ***"Do what makes you happy, be with those who make you smile, and laugh as much as you breathe."***
>
> **—Rachel Ann Nunes**

ATTITUDE 22

Being Comfortable in One's Skin

Being comfortable in one's own skin is another significant attitude that happy people possess. They are open and honest about their weaknesses and strengths, presenting themselves genuinely and authentically. To develop this attitude and find happiness, you can start by listing your strengths and weaknesses on a piece of paper. Acknowledge that weaknesses are a natural part of being human and that it's entirely acceptable to share them with others. In fact, sharing weaknesses is an essential step in overcoming them.

It's important not to label weaknesses as insurmountable limitations. The human mind is incredibly adaptable, and with the right coaching and learning tools, you can improve in areas where you have weaknesses. While contemporary management thinking often emphasises focusing on strengths, there is value in working on areas where you may have weaknesses. Becoming well-rounded and more efficient is a worthy goal.

Happy and successful individuals understand that weaknesses don't define them, nor do they have to be permanent. By addressing areas that matter to them, they can make positive changes and grow as individuals. Furthermore, this philosophy extends to how they view others. They practice acceptance and refrain from quick judgements.

It's essential to apply this attitude not only to ourselves but also to our teams, children, and the people around us. Offering unconditional love and support, assuring them that we cherish and love them for who they are, promotes self-confidence and growth in others. This attitude of acceptance and encouragement creates a positive environment where everyone can thrive.

ATTITUDE 23

Taking it One Day at a Time

Taking life one day at a time with proper planning is another attitude common among happy people, and one that we should strive to develop. Success is achieved by consistently doing something well over time and continually improving. Often, we become preoccupied with worries about the future or dwelling on past shortcomings and failures, neglecting to invest our full attention in the present moment.

It's crucial to understand that the present is what's real, the past exists as memories, and the future remains largely beyond our control. When we adopt the mindset of living one day at a time, we can go to bed each night feeling satisfied and content, knowing that we gave our best effort that day.

Indeed, life is a marathon, and just like in a long race, we must pace ourselves to maintain our health and well-being. It's essential to strike a balance between our ambitions and taking care of ourselves, both mentally and physically. By living one day at a time with proper planning, we can navigate life's challenges while ensuring we are on a sustainable path to success and happiness.

This attitude, when practiced consistently over time, not only leads to success but also brings daily happiness.

Each day becomes an opportunity to give it our all, leaving no stone unturned. By focusing on the present moment and doing our best, we create a fulfilling and satisfying life, one day at a time.

CONCLUSION

In the first chapter, we delved into the significance of having a purpose in life for eternal happiness. We explored the importance of setting meaningful goals that align with our passions, skills and provide value to the world, while being financially rewarding. However, we realised that the journey towards these goals is just as vital as reaching the destination.

Throughout this chapter, we have uncovered various attitudes and qualities that are essential for maintaining happiness on the journey towards our goals. We've learned that happiness is not merely about achieving a goal, but about dealing with life's challenges systematically, leading to a sense of calm, bliss, focus, serenity, peace, and happiness. These attitudes and qualities can be cultivated through consistent efforts, practice, and heightened awareness.

As we conclude this chapter, it's important to remember that you can choose the attitudes and qualities that resonate with you the most and work on them gradually, one at a time. Building happiness is akin to training a muscle, and overexertion can lead to fatigue. Just as a well-groomed and fit individual masters various gym equipment over time, you can develop your unique toolkit for happiness. In the next chapter, we will explore practices that can potentially derail our happiness and strategies to consciously avoid them. I encourage you to embark on this journey of self-improvement and find the attitudes that work best for you, ultimately leading you to lasting happiness.

KEY TAKEAWAYS

Here are the key takeaways from the chapter, organised into 23 distinct attitudes:

1. **Don't Worry:** Focus on positivity and proactive problem-solving rather than worrying about uncontrollable factors.
2. **Be Optimistic and Stay Positive:** Cultivate a positive outlook, practice gratitude, and appreciate life's blessings.
3. **Live Unhurriedly:** Prioritise tasks and avoid multitasking to fully immerse in and enjoy each activity.
4. **Develop Good Habits:** Establish routines that promote physical, mental and spiritual well-being, and balance work with personal life.
5. **Practice Negative Visualization:** Prepare mentally for worst-case scenarios to handle them more effectively.
6. **Prioritize the Important Over the Urgent:** Focus on tasks that align with long-term goals rather than just urgent tasks.
7. **Focus on What You Can Control:** Concentrate on efforts in areas within your control and let go of what you can't control.
8. **Appreciate Imperfection:** Accept and find value in imperfection in oneself, others, and situations.
9. **Redefine Success and Failure:** View success in broader terms, appreciating small victories, and learning from failures.
10. **Seek Learning Opportunities:** Embrace challenges as opportunities for growth and learning.
11. **Be a Lifelong Learner:** Continuously seek knowledge and self-improvement.
12. **Take Responsibility:** Own your actions and their consequences and avoid blaming others.
13. **Embrace Hard Work:** Understand that success requires effort and dedication.

14. **Stop Judging:**   Recognise and accept your situation, and stop judging at every step.
15. **Do Whatever It Takes:**   Persist through setbacks and maintain determination in the face of adversity.
16. **Play to Your Strengths:**   Choose paths where your talents and passions align for a greater chance of success.
17. **Develop a Strong Foundation:**   Invest in building foundational skills and knowledge for long-term success.
18. **Stay Objective:**   Make decisions based on rational thinking rather than emotions.
19. **Give Your Best Always:**   Approach every task with full effort and commitment.
20. **Be Humble:**   Maintain humility and openness to learning and collaboration.
21. **Stop Blaming, Start Doing:**   Focus on actionable steps rather than blaming external factors.
22. **Be Comfortable in Your Own Skin:**   Accept your strengths and weaknesses, and work on improving them.
23. **Take It One Day at a Time:**   Focus on the present, plan adequately, and avoid worrying about the past or future.

These attitudes emphasise a balanced approach to life, where the process and journey are as important as the destination. They encourage personal growth, resilience, and a positive outlook, contributing to a fulfilling and happy life.

> ***"The secret of happiness is not in doing what one likes, but in liking what one does."***
>
> **—James M. Barrie**

CHAPTER 3

AVOIDING THE PRACTICES THAT DERAIL HAPPINESS

INTRODUCTION:

So far in the previous chapters, we have seen 2 things in our search for happiness. We need to understand and find our flow, and find our purpose too.

And once we find our flow and purpose, we should focus on doing our duty with utmost perfection and dedication.

In chapter 2, we saw that even if we find our flow and sense of purpose in life, we must develop a certain set of attitudes while we go about achieving this purpose so that we don't derail our happiness in the process.

What we enjoy doing consistently, day after day, over many years, will help us develop the expertise to achieve success and derive happiness. That happiness will be experienced not only from the success, but also from the journey.

In this chapter, we will look at certain practices that we must avoid, which, if followed, will derail our sense of happiness. The first step is to recognise them, and then the next step is to mitigate them so that we do not derail our happiness, or in other words, shoot ourselves in the foot.

A word of caution.

These practices and habits are not that easy to overcome because it is in our inherent nature, as we will see in this chapter, to behave in a certain way. The same set of habits, if argued, can be helpful to us too, to be successful in some way or another.

We must recognise that these practices, while they derail happiness, have their merits too. But for a long-term, sustainable sense of happiness and accomplishment, we need to learn how to mitigate them and avoid them.

Because there are always other ways to achieve our purpose on the right path, we need to follow the right path and not just any path, and fall into the default way the mind works.

So, let us get started;

LACK OF PERSPECTIVE

There is one habit that we must try to recognise and make conscious steps to inculcate in our decision-making. The best way to lead our life is to develop a sense of perspective in whatever we do, as well as a sense of proportion. Now, what does that mean? In other words, we need to develop a sense of balance.

Let us start exploring this further by talking about the **Marshmallow Experiment**. Marshmallow is a soft sweet made of sugar, egg, and gelatin that feels soft and elastic when chewed.

MARSHMALLOW EXPERIMENT

Now, one may be familiar with the classic example of the Marshmallow Experiment. If you have not come across this experiment, then I would urge you to search it on YouTube and go through the first video that comes up.

The Marshmallow experiment, in short, is an experiment that psychologists conducted on small children.

The experiment began by bringing each child into a private room, sitting them down in a chair and placing a marshmallow on the table in front of them. At this point, the researcher offered a deal to the child.

The researcher told the child that he was going to leave the room and that if the child did not eat the marshmallow while he was away, then they would be rewarded with 2 more marshmallows.

However, if the child decided to eat the first one before the researcher came back, then they would not get a second marshmallow.

So the choice was simple: one treat right now or 2 treats later. The researcher left the room for 15 minutes. As you can imagine, the footage of the children waiting alone in the room was rather entertaining. Some kids jumped up and ate the first marshmallow as soon as the researcher closed the door. Others wiggled, bounced, and fidgeted in their chairs as they tried to restrain themselves but eventually gave in to temptation a few minutes later. And finally, a few of the children did manage to wait the entire time.

This popular study became known as the Marshmallow Experiment, but it wasn't the treat that made it famous. The interesting part came years later.

THE POWER OF DELAYED GRATIFICATION

As the years rolled on and the children grew up, the researchers conducted follow-up studies and tracked each child's progress in several areas. What they found was surprising. The children who were willing to delay gratification and waited to receive the second marshmallow ended up having higher SAT scores, lower levels of substance abuse, a lower likelihood of obesity, better responses to stress, better social skills as reported by their parents, and generally better scores in a range of other life measures.

The researchers followed each child for more than 40 years, and over and over again, the group who waited patiently for the second marshmallow succeeded in whatever capacity they were measuring. In other words, this series of experiments proved that the ability to delay gratification was critical for success in life.

And if you look around, you'll see this playing out everywhere...

- If you delay the gratification of watching television and get your homework done now, then you'll learn more and get better grades.
- If you delay the gratification of buying desserts and chips at the store, then you'll eat healthier when you get home.
- If you delay the gratification of finishing your workout early and put in a few more exercises, then you'll be stronger.

...and countless other examples.

So, from this experiment, we conclude that it is important to have and develop a long-term, strong sense of patience and allow delayed gratification. When we wait and do not immediately look at our life from a short-term perspective, we are ultimately rewarded with much more important things in life.

Ninety percent of the problems and hassles in this world are because everyone wants to get rich and successful in an instant, and for that, they choose the wrong path. For a few days or months, they are basking in their momentary happiness, but it doesn't sustain for long.

The same is true for people who are obese and looking for weight loss. Instead of exercising and controlling their diets, or charting a proper diet plan, they depend on the various medicines which assure them success in a short time frame.

They don't want to follow the tougher and tedious path, but they want results in a short span, which mostly end in failure. They feel happy and elated at the short-term success, but it turns out to be a slap on their face when they encounter obesity relapse. Many even fall prey to the side effects of such medicines.

What is the purpose of having short-term happiness or success, which ultimately leads people to the abyss of failure and depression?

Hence, if you are looking for eternal happiness and prosperity, then focus on the efforts required, which will ultimately lead to the goal and fruitful results.

HARVARD REUNION

In Clayton Christensen's renowned book, *How Will You Measure Your Life?*, Professor Christensen, one of Harvard Business School's top professors, shares a compelling story about his reunions with his college classmates. Despite being some of the most intelligent and capable individuals, many of his batchmates grew increasingly unhappy over the years. Some faced divorces, and others even ended up in jail due to corporate wrongdoings, with only a few finding happiness over time. Professor Christensen pondered, "How come people who are so intelligent ended up not being successful and not being happy?" These were individuals who had achieved tremendous success upon graduating from one of the world's best colleges, yet they still found themselves unfulfilled. This story highlights a crucial aspect of life: the importance of understanding that true happiness doesn't come from immediate rewards, as suggested by the Marshmallow Experiment. It's not about waiting for more marshmallows, but about realising that genuine contentment stems from deeper, more meaningful sources beyond just professional achievements.

Happiness doesn't necessarily come from enjoying the marshmallows after a long wait, nor should it be derived from the short-term gratification that Professor Clayton's batchmates pursued by prioritising their work above all else. These individuals believed they would find happiness once they were rich and successful, but many ended up losing everything because they ignored their health, relationships, family, and ethics.

Happiness should be our priority, and to achieve it, we must maintain perspective and balance in our lives. Just like a car that requires all 4 wheels to be properly balanced to run smoothly, we cannot expect our lives to run well if we only focus on one or 2 aspects. Our happiness cannot depend on a single facet of life, as this is akin to trying to drive a car on one wheel.

To lead a happy and fulfilling life, we need to maintain a sense of balance by focusing on various important aspects: our relationships, spiritual well-being, health, mindset, and overall well-being. This holistic approach is crucial for achieving our goals in life, as discussed in the first chapter. It's neither beneficial to lack a purpose nor to blindly chase one while neglecting other critical elements, such as health and relationships.

By focusing on all key aspects of life in a balanced manner, we can cultivate lasting happiness. This practice of balance is essential for achieving eternal happiness and should be consistently integrated into our daily lives.

"Those who are not looking for happiness are the most likely to find it because those who are searching forget that the surest way to be happy is to seek happiness for others."
—**Martin Luther King Jr.**

SO WHY DO WE LOSE PERSPECTIVE IN LIFE?

The main reason we lose perspective and end up making poor decisions in life is that we hold many inherently flawed beliefs that we must start to question. Our behaviour is influenced by our belief system and values; thus, to change our behaviour, we need to question and transform the underlying beliefs we hold.

The first belief to challenge is the notion that our goals are the most important aspect of life and that we must do whatever it takes to achieve them. This belief often leads us to become frantic and single-minded in our pursuit of success. We hear many successful people recounting how they worked tirelessly, forsaking rest and compromising on important aspects of life to reach their goals. These stories emphasise the sacrifices made to achieve success.

However, we must understand that in this mad race, putting everything else at stake often results in losing it all, including our balance. For every story of someone who achieved their goals through relentless sacrifice, there are stories of those who compromised their values and ended up unhappy, or even facing dire consequences. Conversely, there are also stories of individuals who have achieved great success without sacrificing their health, relationships, and core values.

A prime example is Barack Obama, one of the finest Presidents of the United States. He demonstrated that it is possible to focus on work while also going on planned vacations, maintaining his health, and nurturing a great relationship with his family. Obama exemplifies a highly successful leader who did not compromise his personal life, yet managed to handle the top office in the United States with grace and effectiveness.

By looking at such examples, we learn that it is not necessary to sacrifice everything important in the pursuit of our goals. Maintaining a balance in life, focusing on health, relationships, and personal well-being, while still achieving professional success, is possible. This balanced approach not only leads to achieving our goals, but also ensures that we remain happy and fulfilled throughout our journey.

NEVER EITHER THIS OR THAT

Life doesn't need to be a choice between A or B. We often forget that it's possible to have both. We can be successful and also enjoy great health, nurturing relationships, and pursue other interests that bring us joy. It's about integrating all aspects of life rather than sacrificing one for the other.

Another strongly held misconception is the belief that we will be happy only if we are rich, successful, or have numerous degrees to showcase. This belief is far from the truth. We need to question this notion because happiness is not a destination achieved by wealth or fame, according to societal standards.

Happiness is something we can experience today. Continuously chasing something in anticipation of future happiness sets us up for disappointment because, once we reach one milestone, we find there are still more to conquer. It becomes a never-ending cycle. True happiness is found not at the summit, but in the journey to reaching it.

Happiness is like a butterfly; if you chase it, it flies away. But if you sit calmly and enjoy what you are doing, it comes and rests on your shoulder. The only way to experience happiness throughout our journey is by maintaining balance and perspective in our lives. By appreciating the process and staying grounded, we can find joy in each step we take, ensuring that our pursuit of success doesn't come at the cost of our well-being and contentment.

"It is good to have money and the things that money can buy, but it's good too to check up once in a while and make sure you haven't lost the things money can't buy."

—George Lorimer

PRIORITISING EXTERNAL VALIDATION

A colleague of mine once obsessed over his Fitbit, proudly announcing his step count every day. After one meeting, he bragged about hitting 10,000 steps before lunch. Someone joked, "Is your Fitbit promoting you now?"—and the room burst into laughter. It highlighted how much he craved external validation, a trait that can derail happiness. While praise can motivate, relying on it too much can lead us astray. True well-being comes from within, not from others' approval.

The continuous need for external validation can manifest as a desire for promotions, the need to show off power, flaunting superiority, or endlessly chasing riches to feel happy. Scientifically, it is true that others' praises influence our behaviour. When someone praises us, we feel more motivated, and this validation helps us master our tasks and achieve our goals. Such comparisons can give us a sense of direction and progress.

While external validation can be a useful tool for assessing our progress, an obsessive focus on it can derail our sense of well-being and happiness in the long run. This is a trait we must recognise and consciously avoid. Our sense of well-being and self-worth should stem from within, not from how others judge us. World-class performers and athletes often focus intensely on their tasks and may be misjudged by others for not fitting in with common expectations.

People tend to prefer individuals who fit into conventional moulds, but those aiming for world-class performance or unique missions often do not conform to these norms. This non-conformity can jeopardise their chances of excelling in their chosen fields if they seek external validation from the wrong sources. Therefore, one of the key strategies to avoid falling into the trap of seeking external validation is to align our goals with like-minded people or institutions where we spend most of our time.

If we find a lack of alignment, it is crucial to seek out a different cohort or company of people. Our company should consist of like-minded individuals who appreciate us for who we are and create an environment where we can thrive. These people should mentor and support us in becoming better versions of ourselves, fostering an atmosphere where we can work in our own space and at our own pace.

By surrounding ourselves with a supportive network and focusing on intrinsic motivation, we can cultivate a sustainable sense of well-being and happiness. This balanced approach ensures that our drive for success does not overshadow our need for genuine, lasting contentment.

"When one door of happiness closes, another opens, but often we look so long at the closed door that we do not see the one that has been opened for us."

—Helen Keller

DISTRUSTING THE WORLD

The third habit that can severely undermine our happiness and well-being is the tendency to distrust the entire world. Over-anxious individuals often exhibit this behaviour. For example, consider a new employee who is perpetually anxious, believing he won't be able to deliver and that someone is out to get him. This mindset challenges the entire recruitment process. The question arises: "Why would they recruit him in the first place if they wanted to fire him immediately without evaluating his performance?"

This distrust stems from the belief that someone is always trying to undermine us. Constantly focusing on worst-case scenarios tortures our well-being because we are consumed by negative thoughts. And it is true that if we are continuously thinking of negative things, they seem to be attracted to us, leading to negative outcomes.

An easy counter-argument is that if we are too trusting, others might take advantage of us. It might not be prudent to maintain a high level of trust. However, I am not suggesting we should be gullible or lack perspective. Our initial approach to the world should be one of trust. There are indeed people out there who might cheat us, but as we learn to trust others, we become better at sensing dishonesty. If we sense dishonesty or identify someone with a history of deceit, we can recognise these traits and avoid such individuals.

It's okay to be taken for a ride occasionally because that's how we learn. If we maintain a negative mindset and distrust everyone, it will erode our joy and keep us under constant pressure.

Here, I would like to reference the Pygmalion effect: if we trust our children or workers, they are encouraged to work hard, develop faster, and perform well. Conversely, if we don't trust them, their performance suffers. If a teacher distrusts her students or a boss distrusts his employees, their performance drops. To be happy, we must start from a viewpoint of trust. We must have positive thinking toward the world. When we tell our team and our children that we trust them and are there for them, we set a high benchmark of expectation. This creates an environment where people want to join us and work alongside us, and it brings tremendous peace and joy to our hearts.

The best way to develop this attitude is to ask: "What is the worst thing that can happen in a particular situation?" and take a calculated risk. Once we have taken the risk, we should not continuously worry and fret over the situation. It's okay to lose a few battles because, to win something, we have to lose something. If we fail in our judgement, so what? At least, we were happy, and we should embrace the situation as a learning opportunity.

"There is only one cause of unhappiness: the false beliefs you have in your head, beliefs so widespread, so commonly held that it never occurs to you to question them."
—Anthony de Mello

SAYING NO TO OTHERS, ONESELF, AND LIFE

One of the practices that we must avoid, which derails our sense of happiness, is continuously saying 'No' to others, to oneself, and to life. At the heart of this habit lies our lack of trust in ourselves, others, and life in general. Let us examine this further.

What does it mean to say 'No' to oneself?

Many people consciously avoid being happy or feeling good about themselves. When we explore the reasons behind this, we often find that they lack confidence in a particular situation and feel unworthy. To counter this, we need to remind ourselves: "Everyone born into this world is endowed with unique skills, and with the right coaching and peer group, anyone can achieve what they set out to do." By feeling unworthy or lacking confidence, how can we expect others to trust us? Trust originates from self-confidence, our belief in our vision, and our ability to grow.

Saying 'No' to others:

The moment someone asks for help, individuals who are not content with themselves often respond with a 'No.' Why do they do this? It could be due to selfishness, self-centredness, lack of time, distrust of others, or misconceptions about others. They might feel that people will take advantage of them or be too stressed about their own lives. Consequently, others stop asking for their help, cease to collaborate, and avoid interaction, considering them selfish. Humans are inherently social beings; we need others for psychological support. The greatest punishment for a prisoner is solitary confinement. Loneliness, more than the harsh environment, drives people insane.

By saying 'No' to ourselves, our aspirations, and others' needs for support, we lose opportunities in life. Playing it too safe results in losing much-needed social support and numerous excellent platforms. Additionally, we miss out on experiences that could help us grow, learn new skills and understand different cultures. Therefore, this is a quality we must avoid to be happy.

The best approach is to say 'Yes' to ourselves and others. Ask: "What is the probability that the person I am going to say 'No' to will do something bad?", "What is the probability that the person asking for my help will exploit me?" Even if we are unsure how to assess the probability, we should learn to take a chance. "What is the worst thing that can happen if we extend a helping hand?" How badly could I be hurt in such a situation? Reflect on past instances when we have given unconditional help or love; those experiences likely helped us grow and strengthened our relationships.

What if we were in a similar situation?

Imagine your car breaks down on a highway, and you are stranded. A stranger stops to help tow your car or takes you to the nearest garage. What if no one stopped, leaving you stranded for hours? Even imagining this scenario is unsettling. Hence, we must pay it forward by helping others in need. Measure each day not by achievements and awards, but by how many people we have helped and who benefited from our help.

Ask: "How many people have I helped without expecting anything in return?" Continuously train our minds to focus outwardly. Once we start saying 'Yes' to the world, we will discover immense joy in helping others and bringing smiles to their faces. Helping others doesn't always mean materially; it can be a kind word, a simple thank you, or appreciating someone's presence in our lives. This motivates us to say 'Yes' to others.

For those who distrust the world:

Consider a small risk management framework. While not everyone can be trusted, start with small favours, not large ones. Observe if the person reciprocates. Ask yourself, "Are they equally altruistic?" If the answer is yes, proceed to extend more help to them. This approach allows us to build trust gradually and fosters a positive and supportive environment, ultimately contributing to our happiness and well-being.

> *"The more you praise and celebrate your life,*
> *the more there is in life to celebrate."*
>
> —Oprah Winfrey

PUTTING THE CART BEFORE THE HORSE

Another significant derailer of happiness is our misguided expectations or incorrect assessment of reality. If we lack self-awareness, we will perpetually misjudge our ability to handle situations. This often leads to prioritising tasks that shouldn't be undertaken at that moment, metaphorically putting the cart before the horse.

It's essential to recognise that achieving excellence in any field requires 10,000 hours of consistent, focused effort. Patience and persistence are key. Overextending ourselves and attempting to take on more than we can handle only adds unnecessary pressure, especially when we are not yet prepared to perform at a high level. This pressure erodes our happiness. We must accept that good things in life take time to materialise.

Constantly comparing ourselves to others who seem to achieve success more quickly can be detrimental. By lacking perspective and making such comparisons, we set ourselves up for disappointment and misery. It's crucial to prioritise and accurately assess situations.

In a new organisation, young teams often face immense pressure, leading them to crack under the strain. Expecting immediate revenue from a nascent team is akin to asking a child to run a marathon. Most start-ups, despite having brilliant ideas and ample funding, fail due to unrealistic expectations and an urgency for quick results. This ruins their promising future. Expecting a seed to grow into a tree overnight is futile and detrimental. Trees take years to develop, just as it takes 10,000 hours of dedicated effort to master a craft and 10 years of hard work to build a sustainable business.

By focusing on hard work rather than the time it takes, we can remain relaxed and resilient in the face of challenges. Understanding that expertise and success require time allows us to persevere without giving up at the first sign of difficulty.

In conclusion, happiness is a multifaceted state that can be undermined by various habits and mindsets. We must avoid the pitfalls of seeking external validation, distrusting the world, saying 'No' to ourselves and others, and setting unrealistic expectations. By fostering self-confidence, trust, patience, and a willingness to help others, we can cultivate a more fulfilling and joyful life. Remember, happiness is not a destination but a journey, and embracing this journey with an open heart and mind will lead to lasting well-being.

"A ROLLING STONE GATHERS NO MOSS"

We have to stay committed to something to become better at it. A common excuse for not putting in enough effort is that the world is constantly changing. While change is inevitable, we can't allow it to become a habit of shifting focus too often. Once we find something meaningful, we should dedicate ourselves wholeheartedly to it.

This reminds me of a wonderful story about Mahatma Gandhi. A person living in his ashram was attending French classes. One day, Bapuji called him and asked, "Why are you attending French classes? Don't you know that we are dedicated to the freedom movement? I request you to give up your French classes and focus solely on India's freedom." The person gave up her French classes to devote herself entirely to the freedom movement. Such was the commitment of Bapuji to India's freedom.

We must show similar dedication to our chosen tasks, giving our best to ensure we don't put the cart before the horse. Prioritise and understand that life is a marathon, not a sprint.

When our children are growing, we can't pressurise them daily to perform. They are children, after all. We need to give them time to grow and develop their skills, allowing them to make mistakes. The same patience we have for our children should be extended to all tasks we undertake.

"Why don't we carry the same attitude for all the people we meet?" Let them make mistakes, let them learn and grow, be patient, and help them understand. We must allow people to perform and improve without constantly putting ourselves and everyone else under pressure. Life is long, and as we become better at what we do, things will start looking more optimistic, and we will achieve perfection in our endeavours.

Patience is essential. Rushing the process only leads to unnecessary stress and setbacks. By staying committed, giving our best, and allowing time for growth and development, we can achieve our goals and find fulfilment in our efforts.

EXPECTING THAT WE ARE/SHOULD BE RIGHT ALL THE TIME

Another practice that significantly derails happiness is the expectation that we should be right all the time. This expectation is, when you think about it, quite unreasonable. It's simply not possible for us or our teams to always be correct.

First, we must understand and accept that no one in this world is perfect. Since perfection is unattainable, we also have the right to be imperfect. While we should strive for excellence and try to achieve the highest standards in our chosen fields, it's equally important to acknowledge that we won't always reach perfection. Implementing this mindset can be challenging, especially as we gain experience and skills, which naturally boost our confidence. However, there's a very fine line between confidence and hubris.

Jack Welch, in his book *Straight From the Gut*, discusses his approach to recruitment, revealing that he accepts being wrong about half the time. For one of the world's most renowned CEOs to admit such humility demonstrates that making mistakes is a common part of the human experience. If we were truly capable of being consistently right, even 60% of the time, we might as well quit our jobs and try to become millionaires in the stock market. But obviously, being right all the time is not feasible.

In the complex world we live in today, maintaining an attitude that expects constant correctness can be not only unrealistic but also dangerous. There are multiple factors and teams involved in any organisational operation, making the path to the desired outcome often far from straightforward.

Moreover, expecting to always be right can impede our happiness. This expectation can be self-imposed, or we might project it onto others, expecting them to perform exactly as we envision. Such expectations are nearly impossible to fulfil and can lead to frustration and disappointment.

Instead of clinging to the need to always be right, we should cultivate a culture of learning and growth. This involves acknowledging our mistakes, learning from them, and understanding that error is part of the human condition. By fostering an environment where mistakes are viewed as opportunities for improvement, rather than failures, we can enhance our personal and professional growth, reduce unnecessary pressure, and, consequently, increase our overall happiness.

> ***"Be happy with what you have***
> ***while working for what you want."***
>
> **—Helen Keller**

If we examine closely the instances where we've been angry with someone, or they with us, it often stems from our expectations that others should behave as we want them to. However, when they act contrary to our desires, not only do our relationships suffer, but we also risk appearing unforgiving and lacking in humility. Many of the world's problems are exacerbated by the inflated egos of those who believe they are flawless, only to realise their fallibility when they find themselves without support.

The attitude we need to adopt is one of accepting our imperfections and the inevitability of making mistakes. By confidently accepting this reality, we can begin to make peace with others and ourselves. It's crucial to recognise that there is always a degree of uncertainty attached to every decision; the probability of achieving a perfect outcome is never 100%.

We can strive to improve the likelihood of success, enhance the quality of our decisions and, with practice, increase the efficiency of repetitive tasks. Consider learning to drive a car: initially, we make many mistakes, but over time, proficiency can become second nature. However, we must acknowledge that it takes time to reach this level of skill, and even experienced drivers can make critical errors.

To manage our expectations and responses effectively, it can be helpful to categorise problems into 2 types. The first type includes problems with known solutions, which can be addressed using our own or someone else's expertise. The second type comprises unknown problems with unknown solutions.

When we categorise problems this way, we achieve a certain clarity. We begin to understand that problems without known solutions require us to adjust our expectations of ourselves, our teams, our bosses, and the world at large. This realisation helps us appreciate the challenges others face in solving these issues, which can lead to a greater sense of empathy and patience.

This categorisation puts our minds at ease, fostering an environment where we remind ourselves that our job is to learn and attempt to solve these problems. It's important to tell ourselves that it's okay to fail and make mistakes, especially when faced with challenging and unfamiliar situations. Embracing this mindset not only helps us grow but also enhances our ability to navigate the complexities of life with greater resilience and understanding.

DESIRE-LESS, GOALLESS, AND JUST COASTING ALONG

Living in a desire-less, goal-less existence is a sure way to kill happiness, and unfortunately, it's a habit I see many people practising today. This trend, often stemming from a misinterpretation of modern philosophy and spiritual texts, advocates for a life of indifference, suggesting that it's better not to be attached to or pursue anything.

I believe that such a life is akin to that of an animal. Observing animals, we notice they don't have goals but live a mechanical existence dictated by instinct and routine. They wake up, go about their day, and fulfil their basic needs without a higher purpose. As humans, however, we have the capacity to understand the purpose of life beyond mere survival. Our purpose should include striving for perfection in our endeavours, achieving self-mastery, understanding ourselves and the world around us, and making meaningful contributions.

A life where we disconnect from desires and the world can become monotonous and lifeless. What is life if devoid of desires? It's healthy to have aspirations. For instance, while some philosophies caution against pursuing material wealth, I argue that there's nothing wrong with desiring material riches, as long as they don't consume us and lead to anxiety. If material wealth motivates us, we should pursue it passionately. Having a goal and chasing it with zeal is far better than a desire-less, goal-less existence. A life without motive and goals is like a canvas with no painting.

The Bhagavad Gita beautifully discusses the 3 Gunas: Rajasik, Tamsik, and Satvik. Satvik is the highest state where one is at peace with oneself, a concept we'll explore further in Chapter 6. The Rajasik guna represents a state of passion and desire, while the Tamsik guna is characterised by a lack of goals and desires. It's better to be Rajasik, with clear goals and the drive to achieve them, rather than Tamsik and lead a goal-less life.

It's important to understand that while the Satvik state represents balance and peace, it should not be confused with a desire-less, goal-less state. Although both might appear similar superficially, they are fundamentally different. Consider a beggar and a sannyasin: both might beg for food, but their underlying motivations differ. The beggar may avoid work despite being capable, representing laziness and a Tamsik state, while the sannyasin has renounced worldly desires for spiritual enlightenment, aiming for a Satvik state.

It's crucial to understand these distinctions. Having goals and desires is not inherently negative, as long as they don't disrupt our peace. Anxiety, for instance, can be a motivator in business, as Andy Grove points out in his book, *Only the Paranoid Survive*. It's acceptable to be concerned about competition, but it becomes problematic if insecurity overwhelms us. Anxiety should not prevent us from stepping onto the stage; instead, it should propel us to perform and achieve the goals we set for ourselves.

**"Who is the happier man, he who has
braved the storm of life and lived, or he who
has stayed securely on shore and merely existed?"**
—Hunter S. Thompson

COGNITIVE DISTORTION

Aristotle insightfully noted that human beings are not necessarily rational, but rather rationalising creatures. This notion is elaborated upon by Nobel laureate Daniel Kahneman in his seminal work, *Thinking, Fast and Slow,* which explores the numerous biases and rational misjudgments that cloud our thinking. Despite our belief in our rationality, research consistently shows that everyone has blind spots, leading to simple yet significant errors.

For instance, a seasoned chess player, due to years of practice and familiarity with the game, can analyse situations on the chessboard with far greater clarity and precision than an amateur. This proficiency comes from developed patterns of thinking and tactics that aid in making judicious decisions within the familiar confines of chess. However, when placed in an unfamiliar situation, even a chess grandmaster may struggle. This is because the decision-making patterns that serve well in chess do not necessarily apply in different contexts.

This highlights an important reality for all of us: we carry a host of cognitive distortions that can impede rational decision-making. Furthermore, our reactions and behaviours are often based on the optimistic belief that we can handle situations effectively. We tend to attribute our responses to external events, but in reality, no 2 people react the same way to the same event. This variance is because our belief systems act as filters through which we interpret the world, shaping our reactions uniquely.

Therefore, to achieve happiness and discover true bliss in life, we must critically examine the deep-seated beliefs that skew our interpretation of the world. If our belief systems are flawed, and we continue to adhere to them without question, leading a happy life becomes a formidable challenge.

The path to improvement involves questioning our beliefs and biases and embracing humility in the face of varying situations. Even the most logical and brilliant minds are susceptible to mistakes. Acknowledging the possibility that we might be wrong is a crucial step. We must ensure that our belief system does not obstruct our path to happiness by fostering misery and unhappiness. By adopting a more reflective and open-minded approach, we can mitigate the impact of our biases and enhance our overall well-being.

DON'T ASSUME

A classic mistake many of us make is assuming that we fully understand a situation and believing that others are purposefully not supporting us. To move beyond this erroneous assumption, the first step is direct communication.

For instance, when we perceive that others are not assisting us, we often concoct reasons why, based on our assumptions. A more effective approach is to directly approach the person and express our need for help, rather than speculating about their motives. Additionally, we often worry that others might think poorly of us or misinterpret our actions. These fears are usually unfounded, and it's crucial to avoid making assumptions and instead seek to validate our thoughts through open communication.

The Johari Window model, created by American psychologists Joseph Luft and Harry Ingham, serves as an insightful tool for understanding our own self-awareness and the perceptions of others. This model highlights 4 key areas:

- Open Area: Aspects of ourselves that both we and others know.

- Blind Spot: Traits that others see in us, but we are unaware of.
- Hidden Area: Traits that we know about ourselves, but others do not.
- Unknown Area: Traits that neither we nor others are aware of.

The Johari Window underscores the importance of not assuming. It suggests that we often overlook the underlying belief systems and values driving another person's behaviour, leading to misunderstandings. By being open and acknowledging that we might not fully understand the reasons behind someone's actions, we foster clearer communication.

We must consider that others may not share our values, cultural background, or experiences. Opening up and sharing our stories helps others understand our actions and intentions. This dialogue can enlighten us about aspects of our personality that we were previously unaware of and help others gain insight into our character.

Building trust, community, and friendships begins with discarding assumptions about others based on our personal values. Instead, we should strive for clarity by understanding that people's actions are shaped by their unique belief systems.

Thus, we should not only refrain from making assumptions but also proactively ask for clarity. Moreover, offering help, even when it has not been requested, and maintaining openness and transparency can strengthen relationships. Being explicit and straightforward in our communications helps prevent misunderstandings and misinterpretations, paving the way for more genuine and trusting interactions.

> *"Of all the means to ensure happiness throughout the whole life, by far, the most important is the acquisition of friends."*
>
> **—Epicurus**

TAKING EXTREME POSITIONS

Another cause of unhappiness is that we often subject ourselves to very extreme positions, both in our internal dialogues and in explanations we provide to others about why certain situations arise. For instance, one might take the entire blame upon themselves, leading to continuous self-reproach, such as, "I am the one who has caused this problem." This mindset can significantly erode our happiness, make us miserable, and diminish our confidence.

Alternatively, we might force ourselves to adopt someone else's viewpoint, which can undermine our self-esteem and self-worth. Even if we don't overtly admit to others that we blame ourselves, internally accepting responsibility for causing distress to another person can be damaging. Conversely, a common opposing extreme is to blame every adverse situation on someone else's incapacity or poor attitude. This often results in anger towards others, leading to rudeness and, ultimately, damaging our relationships.

Once relationships are strained or broken, we may start feeling isolated, compounding our unhappiness. It's crucial to recognise that most situations arise from a complex interplay of factors. Some of these factors are external, beyond our control, while others may be influenced by our actions. Recognising this complexity is essential.

Therefore, it's vital to adopt a balanced view and avoid taking extreme positions. By doing so, we can prevent the twin pitfalls of internal misery and causing distress to others. Adopting a balanced approach helps us understand that while we may contribute to certain outcomes, other elements are also at play, many of which are beyond our individual control.

Embracing this balanced perspective allows us to approach situations with a more nuanced understanding, reducing the tendency to swing towards extreme self-blame or undue criticism of others. This approach not only preserves our mental well-being but also helps maintain healthier relationships. By avoiding extremes and striving for balance, we can escape the trap of allowing extreme viewpoints to lead to misery and unhappiness.

THINKING CHALLENGES ALL THE TIME

Continually dwelling on the challenges we face is another surefire way to diminish our happiness. As the adage goes, "Successful and happy people don't always keep on thinking about the challenges." Instead, they focus on actionable steps rather than ruminating over the obstacles they encounter. This pattern of constantly worrying about difficulties represents a mental trap that can lead to anxiety and a feeling of helplessness.

To counter this mindset, a useful approach is to ask, "Is there another way to deal with this problematic situation?" If we only fixate on the challenges, they begin to erode our abilities and shake our self-confidence. We might start to feel that the situation is hopeless and that we are incapable of resolving the issues we face.

A positive trait I've observed in happy individuals is their ability to explore different methods of handling a situation or seeking advice from others. By inviting solutions and perspectives from various sources, we can broaden our view of the problem. This not only brings diverse insights but also reduces the emotional weight of carrying the burden alone.

Once we shift our focus from dwelling on the problems to actively seeking solutions, we start to see the silver lining. Instead of feeling gloomy and overwhelmed, we feel energised to work towards resolving the issue. This proactive approach transforms our perspective, turning seemingly insurmountable challenges into manageable tasks.

Additionally, looking for the silver lining helps us maintain a positive outlook, essential for navigating through tough times. By viewing challenges as opportunities to grow and learn, we harness the power of positivity, which fuels our progress and aids in overcoming obstacles. This mindset not only preserves our happiness but also propels us toward achieving our goals, proving that the way we choose to face our difficulties can define our success and contentment in life.

Embracing the ethos of "When life throws lemons at you, make lemonade" encourages us to see opportunities in our challenges. A powerful technique in managing these situations is to ask ourselves, "What is the worst thing that can happen?" By mentally preparing for the worst-case scenario, we can reduce the fear associated with it. This preparation not only mitigates anxiety but also helps shift our perspective towards a more optimistic outlook, enhancing our chances of success.

In the rapid analysis of situations, it's easy to spiral into a chain reaction where one problem leads to another, creating what feels like an avalanche of issues. By stepping back and approaching the problem with a general strategy, we can develop a range of potential solutions, building our confidence to tackle the challenge head-on.

However, focusing too much on the complexity of a situation can lead to paranoia and excessive stress. When overwhelmed, the best course of action is to take a break. If that's not possible, it's helpful to reflect and ask, "How often have the scenarios I fear actually occurred? What is the likelihood they will happen again?" Assigning a realistic probability to these fears allows us to methodically evaluate and manage them.

In life, risk is inherent, and our minds often overestimate risk due to the unknown nature of challenging situations.

To address this, it's essential to think rationally about the risks involved and consult with experts who have experience with similar challenges. These experts can provide valuable insights, helping us to better understand and manage the situation.

Knowledge is key in navigating challenges effectively. Seeking expertise not only informs us about the potential risks but also about how to approach them wisely. It's crucial to recognise that no situation is entirely risk-free; our goal should be to manage and minimise risk, not to eliminate it entirely. The probability of completely avoiding risk is never 100%, but with the right approach and mindset, we can significantly reduce it.

By accepting that each action and decision carries some degree of risk, we can condition our minds to handle challenges more comfortably. This acceptance allows us to remain calm and focused, helping us to make more informed decisions and, ultimately, to navigate through life's challenges more effectively. Thus, the journey involves continuously learning to balance risk, seeking knowledge and expertise, and adjusting our strategies as needed to deal with whatever challenges arise.

Continuing to invest in actions, even when faced with potential setbacks, is crucial. Every decision carries some level of risk, and by conditioning our minds to accept and manage these risks, we empower ourselves to persevere and overcome challenges. Much like athletes who train not just physically but mentally, visualising various scenarios and outcomes, we too can adopt a proactive mindset that prepares us for different possibilities.

When facing a complex situation, a structured approach can be immensely helpful. Start by identifying all possible outcomes that might arise from the situation. Assign a probability to each outcome based on past experiences, data, or other evidence. This methodical assessment helps you to not only anticipate but also prepare for various scenarios, thereby reducing uncertainty and anxiety.

Preparation involves crafting creative solutions for each potential outcome. By having a contingency plan in place, you are less likely to be caught off guard and more likely to handle challenges with confidence and agility. This strategic approach does not just apply to mitigating risks, but also to capitalising on opportunities that may arise during the process.

For instance, if you anticipate a highly stressful situation filled with challenges, don't wait passively for the issues to manifest. Instead, actively prepare by thinking through these challenges in advance. Such preemptive thinking is akin to the mental simulations practiced by athletes. They often visualise themselves encountering various challenges during their performance, which prepares them to react more effectively when those situations actually occur. This mental preparation not only boosts their confidence but also enhances their ability to perform under pressure.

This strategy is supported by research showing that mental simulation can significantly improve performance. By mentally rehearsing how to handle different challenges, individuals can develop a 'mental muscle memory' of sorts, which helps in swiftly navigating complex situations when they arise.

Thus, by adopting a proactive and prepared approach, embracing the inevitability of risks, and equipping ourselves with effective strategies and solutions, we can maintain control over our circumstances. This not only prevents us from being overwhelmed, but also enhances our resilience, enabling us to navigate life's challenges more effectively and maintain our overall happiness.

FEELING OF HELPLESSNESS

One of the major challenges that can derail our happiness is the feeling of helplessness when faced with a difficult or stressful situation. The key piece of advice I can offer is not to give up easily and to take things one step at a time.

For instance, imagine you're running a marathon and you start feeling overwhelming body aches, tempting you to quit. Instead of giving in to this urge, focus on taking one step at a time or even taking smaller, manageable steps. These adjustments can provide some relief, and, gradually, you might find yourself re-energised and ready to continue.

When confronting a particularly daunting challenge, it's crucial not to dwell on the entire future but to tackle it one day at a time. Ask yourself, "How can I make today a bit better than yesterday?" Addressing your situation daily can significantly alleviate feelings of helplessness.

Another effective strategy is to confide in and rely on a supportive circle of friends who can help navigate through tough times. Having someone who listens patiently, understands your struggles, and offers new perspectives can be incredibly comforting and empowering. Often, discussing your challenges openly can help you realise that the solutions may already lie within you. This realisation can shift your perspective, helping you view your situation more objectively, rather than becoming overwhelmed by emotions.

This approach is especially pertinent in situations like tough negotiations, where you might feel outclassed by the other party's skills and resources. It's easy to feel intimidated and presume defeat, but conceding too soon ensures failure. Instead, maintain your involvement in the discussion. By staying engaged, you signal to the other party that you are resilient and not easily overpowered. This persistence often shifts the dynamic, opening up possibilities for a more balanced and mutually beneficial outcome.

Continuously explore the situation and strive for the best possible solutions, aiming for a win-win scenario. Your tenacity and strength in such challenging situations will not only lead to better outcomes but are also likely to earn respect and admiration from others. In doing so, you transform potential setbacks into opportunities for growth and reaffirm your capacity to handle life's challenges effectively.

"I am determined to be cheerful and happy in whatever situation I may find myself. For I have learned that the greater part of our misery or unhappiness is determined not by our circumstance, but by our disposition."

—Martha Washington

CONCLUSION

In this chapter, we delved into various habits and behaviours that can derail our pursuit of lasting happiness. By exploring cognitive distortions, extreme positions, the pitfalls of seeking external validation, and the importance of delayed gratification, we highlighted how these factors can undermine our well-being. We also examined the necessity of maintaining balance, trusting others, and saying 'Yes' to life. By recognising these patterns and actively working on them, we can pave the way for a more fulfilling and joyous life.

KEY TAKEAWAYS

In this chapter, we delved into various habits and behaviours that can derail our pursuit of lasting,

1. **Delayed Gratification:** Embrace the power of patience and the benefits of delaying immediate rewards for long-term success and happiness.

2. **Perspective and Balance:**   Cultivate a balanced approach to life, maintaining perspective in all aspects, including health, relationships, and professional goals.

3. **External Validation:**   Avoid the trap of constantly seeking external validation. Instead, focus on intrinsic motivation and align yourself with supportive, like-minded individuals.

4. **Trust:**   Start from a place of trust rather than distrust, fostering a positive environment that encourages growth and collaboration.

5. **Saying 'Yes':**   Adopt a 'Yes' mindset towards yourself and others, promoting a supportive and connected community.

6. **Realistic Expectations:**   Understand that perfection is unattainable and embrace the process of learning from mistakes, fostering a growth-oriented mindset.

7. **Balanced Viewpoints:**   Avoid taking extreme positions in your internal and external dialogues to maintain mental well-being and healthy relationships.

8. **Solution-Focused Thinking:**   Shift focus from dwelling on challenges to seeking actionable solutions, harnessing positivity, and resilience.

9. **Risk Management:**   Accept that risk is inherent in every decision. By preparing for potential setbacks and seeking expert advice, you can navigate challenges more effectively.

10. **Continuous Effort:**   Persist in your endeavours despite obstacles, taking things one step at a time and seeking support when needed, to overcome feelings of helplessness.

Remember, true happiness is found in the journey, in the balanced pursuit of our goals, and in our relationships with others and ourselves.

CHAPTER 4

Taking Others Along, a Life of Service

INTRODUCTION:

Continuing from the insights and strategies discussed in the previous chapters, this chapter delves into the crucial role of cooperation and social connections in achieving happiness. We've explored finding purpose and embracing flow states in Chapter 1, understanding that the ends do not justify the means in Chapter 2, and identifying detrimental practices that can undermine our happiness in Chapter 3. Now, we turn our focus towards the importance of cultivating and maintaining relationships.

Human beings are inherently social creatures. Isolation, as seen in extreme conditions like solitary confinement in prisons, can have devastating psychological effects, underscoring the essential nature of social interaction. While the need for relationships is intuitively understood, many of us lack formal guidance on how to effectively build and nurture these connections.

Building meaningful relationships requires time and effort, much like cultivating a garden. It's a delicate process that can be easily disrupted by even a small mistake. A minor misunderstanding or a brief moment of neglect can strain, or even sever, bonds, much like a glass vessel that, once cracked, can never be completely restored to its original state. The visible cracks remind us of the fragility of relationships and the care they require.

Therefore, it is paramount to approach relationships with intentionality and care. This involves not only being mindful of how we interact with others but also actively working to foster trust and mutual respect. Here are a few strategies to enhance cooperation and strengthen social bonds:

- Active Listening: Engage genuinely with others, showing interest in their thoughts, feelings, and experiences. This helps build empathy and understanding, forming a solid foundation for lasting relationships.

- Consistent Communication: Maintain regular contact with friends and colleagues. Consistency demonstrates reliability and commitment to the relationship.

- Conflict Resolution: Address misunderstandings and disagreements promptly and respectfully. Avoiding or ignoring conflicts can lead to resentment, which might fester and weaken bonds.

- Mutual Support: Offer help and be willing to ask for it in return. Reciprocal support not only strengthens relationships but also builds a network of resources that can be crucial in times of need.

- Appreciation and Recognition: Regularly express gratitude and appreciation. Acknowledging others' contributions can enhance their sense of self-worth and deepen the connection.

- Shared Experiences: Create opportunities for positive interactions and shared experiences. Whether it's working on a common project, enjoying a hobby together, or celebrating milestones, shared experiences can create lasting memories and strengthen bonds.

By implementing these strategies, we not only improve our social interactions, but also increase our overall happiness. Strong relationships not only provide support and joy, but also enrich our lives with shared experiences and mutual growth.

This chapter underscores the importance of being proactive in building and maintaining relationships as a key component of a fulfilling and happy life.

Maintaining strong relationships is not just about creating connections, but also about sustaining them over the long haul. An incorrect word or insensitive behaviour can quickly erode the trust and affection that might have taken years to build. Therefore, it is crucial that we not only form, but also diligently maintain these bonds.

In this chapter, we delve deeply into the importance of nurturing enduring relationships. Having a robust network of friends, well-wishers, and close family ties plays a critical role in our overall happiness and well-being. These relationships provide support during times of stress, joy during moments of celebration and comfort in periods of sorrow.

One profound truth underscores the importance of these connections: at the end of our lives, it is not our achievements or accolades that we reflect on, but the depth and quality of the relationships we have nurtured. A well-known saying captures this sentiment beautifully: "Do not count your life by the number of years, but by the number of friends you have." This perspective emphasises the significance of relationships over the span of our lives.

This chapter will explore these practices in more detail, offering practical advice on how to implement them in daily life. By committing to these principles, we can ensure that our relationships are not only lasting but also enriching, providing a network of emotional support that enhances every aspect of our lives.

"To lead men, you have to lead them with affection."
—JRD Tata

COMMUNICATE TO BUILD STRONG RELATIONSHIPS

Effective communication is indeed crucial for building and maintaining strong relationships. Research suggests that up to 90 percent of relationship challenges stem from communication failures, whether due to saying too much, too little, or expressing thoughts inappropriately for the emotional context.

When communication is overly forceful or harsh, it can alienate and hurt others, causing potentially irreparable damage. Words have immense power – they can heal or hurt, build up or break down. Crossing boundaries with harsh words can sever ties, sometimes permanently. Conversely, being overly lenient or failing to speak up against wrongs can also be detrimental. It can lead to resentment, misunderstandings, and a breeding ground for further conflict.

For instance, parents who are overly indulgent with their children may fail to set necessary boundaries and instil proper values. This can lead to children who are spoiled and ill-prepared to face challenges later in life. On the other hand, being too strict can stifle a child's development and damage the parent-child relationship.

Communication should strive for a balance – it's about saying the right thing, at the right time, in the right way. Achieving this balance means being assertive without being aggressive, being kind without being overly permissive, and being honest without being hurtful.

Another common issue in communication is resorting to either 'fight' or 'flight' responses. The 'fight' form involves confronting issues in an aggressive or confrontational manner, which can escalate conflicts rather than resolve them. The 'flight' form involves avoiding uncomfortable conversations altogether, which can lead to unresolved issues simmering beneath the surface, only to cause bigger problems down the line.

Effective communication requires active listening, empathy, clear expression of needs and boundaries, and the ability to negotiate and compromise. It also involves recognising when to speak and when to listen. Often, what strengthens a relationship isn't just the ability to articulate one's own thoughts and feelings, but the capacity to understand and validate the emotions of others.

Training oneself to communicate effectively can be challenging, but is immensely rewarding. By improving communication skills, individuals can enhance every aspect of their relationships, making them stronger, more resilient, and more fulfilling. This effort towards mastering communication not only benefits personal and family relationships, but also extends to professional interactions, contributing to overall success and satisfaction in various dimensions of life.

Effective communication must be bidirectional. It's essential to recognise that while we have our perspectives, others have theirs, which are equally valid. Open-mindedness in communication means considering that the best solution might not come solely from one side but could emerge from a collaborative effort. Often, a third, more effective solution might surface through a synthesis of different viewpoints.

Transparent and open communication can lead to discovering these third alternatives, which are frequently superior to what either party could conceive independently. It's vital to remember that while everyone is entitled to their opinions, factual accuracy is not subjective and should always guide discussions.

To communicate effectively, one should focus on presenting facts and maintaining a balanced view of the situation at hand, without becoming entrenched in one's position. Communication isn't just about expressing our thoughts; it's equally about understanding the other person's point of view. The adage that we are given 2 ears and one mouth, so that we might listen more than we speak, holds profound truth in communication.

When listening, we must do so empathetically, striving to understand not just what is being said, but why it is being said in a particular way. This deeper level of engagement helps us to comprehend the underlying emotions, motivations, and contexts driving the other person's communication. By fostering this level of empathy and attentiveness, we can enhance our interactions, leading to more productive and meaningful relationships.

For instance, if someone approaches us and begins shouting, it's crucial not to react impulsively, but to pause and attempt to understand the underlying message they are trying to convey. It's helpful to consider why the person might be behaving aggressively. Perhaps they were raised in an environment where such reactions were commonplace, or maybe they've received incorrect information that has led them to act out of misunderstanding. Alternatively, their anger could be justified by a real error on our part, and their shouting is a direct response to that mistake.

In any case, the key to effective communication, especially in tense situations, is to listen more and speak less. By first understanding the root of the issue, we can address the situation more effectively. This involves laying out the facts clearly before diving into opinions. It's crucial to base our responses on solid information as our behaviour and decisions are influenced by the inputs we have—whether these are facts, values, or other forms of information.

For example, consider a scenario where an employee is requesting a promotion. It's essential to understand why they feel they deserve this advancement. After comprehending their perspective, assess and discuss the factual basis for a decision regarding the promotion and communicate this transparently. Ensuring the other person understands the criteria and model used for making such decisions is critical. This approach helps prevent misunderstandings and makes the communication process clear and open.

Effective communication is not just about exchanging information; it's about building relationships, understanding different perspectives, and navigating conflicts constructively. By honing these skills, we can improve not only our personal interactions but also our professional relationships, leading to better outcomes and a more harmonious environment.

ACTIVE LISTENING AND COLLABORATION

Effective communication begins with empathetic and active listening. This involves truly understanding the other person's viewpoint without prematurely forming judgements or responses, laying a solid foundation for meaningful dialogue.

In emotionally charged situations or when facts are unclear, it's wise to pause before responding. Recognising your own knowledge limitations demonstrates maturity and respect for the conversation's accuracy. You might say, "I appreciate your points, but I'm not fully acquainted with all the details of this situation. Let me take some time to understand the facts better. If you have any additional information that could help, please share it with me so I can form a more informed opinion."

This approach keeps the conversation objective and ensures that conclusions are mutually beneficial and based on thorough understanding. When dealing with topics outside your expertise, seeking additional help or consulting with experts is also prudent. Openness to learning and collaboration can significantly enhance decision-making quality.

Once all relevant information is gathered and perspectives are understood, the next step is brainstorming various alternatives. This phase is crucial and should not be rushed. In our eagerness to assert our views, we might overlook the value of the other person's insights. It's important to recognise that both parties might be trying to assert their perspectives, which can lead to communication breakdown and potential harm to the relationship.

To avoid this, pause after the listening phase. Ensure all facts are considered and openly brainstorm potential solutions. This part of the conversation can be incredibly creative and productive. Many people skip it because they lack a structured communication process.

The hypothesis behind generating possible alternatives is that individuals with different perspectives can create more impactful solutions together than alone. This collaborative approach leads to better outcomes and strengthens relationships by respecting diverse opinions and fostering shared accomplishment.

Adopting a structured communication process enhances interaction effectiveness, making conversations more productive and enjoyable. By prioritising understanding, collaboration, and creative problem-solving, you foster an environment where healthy communication thrives, benefiting everyone involved.

Influencing others effectively involves more than just presenting conclusions; it's about sharing the journey that led to those conclusions. This approach allows others to understand the reasoning behind decisions, fostering empathy and mutual respect. It's far more constructive than bluntly asserting conclusions, which can lead to unnecessary conflict and unproductive bargaining scenarios.

In any negotiation or discussion, gains for one party should not come at the expense of another's self-respect. Through collaborative idea generation—the "third alternative"—it's possible to discover solutions that address the needs and interests of all involved. This method goes beyond simple compromise; it seeks to create value in negotiations by exploring options that might not be immediately apparent but meet each party's underlying interests.

This approach emphasises collective progress and taking others along in achieving personal and shared goals. It begins with fostering a group discussion dynamic, valuing collective thinking over individual dictates. Encouraging a collaborative environment enhances decision-making and strengthens bonds between participants, creating a shared sense of purpose and achievement.

Supporting group discussions, rather than enforcing individual viewpoints, allows for a richer exploration of ideas where each participant can contribute uniquely and feel valued. This inclusivity leads to more innovative and effective solutions as diverse perspectives are considered and integrated.

Ultimately, taking others along on your journey isn't just about reaching a destination; it's about building relationships and fostering a sense of community and mutual respect. By prioritising open communication, respectful negotiations, and collaborative problem-solving, we can enhance our happiness and the well-being of those around us, aligning individual purposes with collective goals.

SERVICE ORIENTATION

Communication not only allows for the free exchange of ideas but also plays a crucial role in rallying support for our missions and building strong, healthy relationships. This foundation is essential when striving to make an impact, whether in a personal or professional context.

The next vital step in building relationships and engaging others effectively is adopting a service-oriented attitude. Adam Grant, a renowned professor at Wharton School of the University of Pennsylvania, discusses this concept in his book *Give and Take*. His research highlights a fascinating paradox about individuals he categorises as "givers"—those who consistently help others. While givers often reach high levels of success, they also risk ending up at the lower end of the success spectrum if they fail to balance their generosity with their own interests.

Grant's insight points out that while givers can achieve significant success, they must manage their giving strategically to avoid being exploited by "takers"—those who take more than they give and rarely reciprocate. This involves being discerning about whom to help and considering the personal costs of giving. It's about helping effectively and sustainably, ensuring that one's generosity does not lead to personal or professional depletion.

Interestingly, Grant's research also shows that giving can yield substantial returns. People who practice regular generosity often receive back much more than they give, in terms of both tangible and intangible benefits. This return on investment can manifest through enhanced networks, increased cooperation, and even financial gains. However, the intrinsic value of giving—how it enriches one's life and aligns with personal values—often surpasses these external rewards.

Therefore, while the habit of giving can propel one up the organisational ladder, its true value lies deeper. Whether or not it leads to professional advancement, giving enriches our lives. This book emphasises that genuine happiness, which is more enduring than material wealth, fame, or power, is the ultimate goal. In the final analysis, the richness of our lives will not be measured by the balance in our bank accounts, but by the quality and depth of our relationships and the joy we've derived from living a life of service.

A life dedicated to service—helping friends, well-wishers, and even strangers—should be pursued unconditionally, without expectation of reciprocation. This approach not only cultivates a sense of fulfilment and happiness, but also builds a legacy of generosity and impact. By embracing this philosophy, we ensure that our moments of happiness are not just fleeting, but form a profound and lasting part of our legacy—a true reflection of a life well-lived.

> ***"The best way to find yourself is to lose yourself in the service of others"***
>
> **—Mahatma Gandhi**

MOVE THE CENTRE OF ATTENTION FROM US TO OTHERS

So far in this chapter, we've emphasised the importance of taking others along on our journey, shifting our focus from self-centred concerns to the needs and perspectives of those around us. In our daily lives, it's all too common to prioritise our own desires and plans, often at the expense of genuinely engaging with others. Whether in casual conversations or formal meetings, many of us are guilty of formulating our next comment rather than truly listening to what is being said. This approach not only limits our own understanding but can also feel dismissive and disrespectful to others, stifling the potential for true collaboration.

To foster a more inclusive and cooperative environment, we must consciously shift our focus from our own agendas to actively considering the needs and desires of others. This practice of altruism isn't just about being charitable or kind; it's about genuinely engaging with the world outside our own perspectives.

Addressing concerns about becoming a pushover or being exploited for our altruistic behaviour is crucial. When I discuss altruism, people often express fear that their kindness will be taken advantage of. To this, I respond, "So what?" Yes, it's true that some may exploit generosity, but should that possibility deter us from living a life aligned with our values? If someone chooses to take advantage of kindness, that is a reflection of their character, not a failing of our generosity. They are the ones who must reckon with the moral implications of their actions.

Choosing to live altruistically does not mean we must accept being mistreated or exploited; rather, it's about not letting the fear of such outcomes prevent us from acting according to our principles. We can practice discernment and set boundaries while still being fundamentally oriented towards helping others. This balance allows us to remain true to our altruistic nature without becoming martyrs.

The potential setbacks of living altruistically are far outweighed by the profound satisfaction and deeper connections that come from genuinely caring for and supporting others. Altruism enriches our lives, making them more meaningful and connected. Even if we encounter a few who might abuse our generosity, the broader impact of our actions creates a ripple effect of positivity and collaboration that extends far beyond individual interactions.

Thus, embracing altruism is not just a personal choice, but a societal benefit, fostering a culture of empathy, understanding, and mutual support that can transform the very fabric of our communities. By living with an outward focus, we contribute to a world that reflects our highest values and aspirations, creating a legacy of kindness and cooperation that lasts well beyond our individual experiences.

Let us then channel our energies towards leading a life marked by altruism – a practice embraced by some of the most successful companies in the world. Take, for example, Microsoft under the leadership of Satya Nadella. Nadella has been vocal about the importance of empathy within the organisation, which has fundamentally transformed how the company operates and engages with both its customers and its own team. This shift towards empathy and collaboration has led to the launch of numerous successful products, marking a period of significant innovation and growth for Microsoft.

Similarly, closer to home, the Tata Group embodies the principle that the community is not merely a stakeholder, but the very purpose of its enterprise. This philosophy has allowed them to build a vast conglomerate of businesses under their umbrella while also earning immense trust from consumers. These examples illustrate that a focus on altruism and empathy can lead to progressive business practices and a strong market presence.

What holds true for these large enterprises can also be applied on a personal level. We should extend our concern not only to other people but to the environment, insects, and other living beings. Often, our focus is inward, directed at our desires or, at best, the well-being of our close family and friends. However, expanding our sphere of concern to include our colleagues, our consumers, and the broader community can enrich our lives significantly.

Each day, ask yourself: "Did I help somebody today? Did I do it unconditionally? Did I do it without expecting anything in return, or did I do it because it was the right thing to do?" Living a life of compassion and actively seeking ways to contribute to the well-being of others can lead to profound peace of mind, strengthen our connections with those around us and help us build lasting relationships.

A life lived altruistically is not just about giving, but also about appreciating. As we sit in our rooms, surrounded by objects that we did not create ourselves, it becomes clear that we are the beneficiaries of the work and generosity of countless others. This realisation should inspire gratitude and a desire to give back, enhancing our appreciation for the interconnectedness of our lives.

While some may argue that such an approach is too idealistic, that we should live selfishly as others do, aiming solely to satisfy our own desires, this perspective overlooks the broader impact of our actions. Societies flourish not just through individual success, but through collective well-being.

True prosperity is not measured merely by economic output, but by the quality of life and the health of the community.

Thus, instead of counting our age by the number of years, let us count it by the number of friends and the quality of our relationships, for these are the true measures of a life well-lived. By living in service to others, we not only enrich our own lives but also contribute to creating a more compassionate and prosperous society.

Every object around us, such as a bottle of water, is the result of countless contributions from various individuals. The clean water inside the bottle and the bottle itself are manufactured through extensive efforts by companies dedicated to delivering quality products. This simple example extends to virtually everything we interact with daily; each item represents the cumulative effort of innovators, workers, and visionaries who came before us. Acknowledging this helps us appreciate the interconnectedness of our lives and the contributions of others, fostering a profound sense of gratitude.

This gratitude isn't just an abstract feeling, but a call to action – it encourages us to give back and pay it forward. Just as we have benefited from the labour and ingenuity of past generations, we have a responsibility to contribute positively to the world and its future.

Our immediate families, particularly parents, often make significant sacrifices, working tirelessly to provide us with education and other necessities within their means. We strive to do the same for our children, ensuring they have better opportunities and lives. However, our responsibilities, and our capacity for impact, do not end at our doorstep.

What about the environment that sustains us, or the animals with whom we share this planet? What about the soldiers guarding our borders and ensuring our safety? Our comfortable lives are made possible not only by family and innovators, but also by these often overlooked contributors.

Thus, our sense of gratitude should not be passive but actively motivate us towards altruism—not just towards our immediate circle, but extending to the broader society and the natural world. By actively contributing to the well-being of our community and environment, we engage in a cycle of mutual benefit that enhances our lives and those of others.

Engaging in these acts of giving not only enriches our lives with happiness and strengthens our bonds with others, but also leads to greater wealth creation. This, in turn, empowers us further, enabling us to extend our reach and impact even more significantly.

In essence, living a life of gratitude and altruism leads to a virtuous cycle. By appreciating what we have and using it as a springboard to give back, we can create a more fulfilling, interconnected and prosperous life for ourselves and future generations. This is the true essence of living—not just existing for ourselves, but thriving through the well-being of others and the world we call home.

> *"I believe compassion to be one of the few things we can practice that will bring immediate and long-term happiness to our lives."*
>
> —Dalai Lama

CONCLUSION

In Chapter 4, we explored the profound impact of cooperation, social connections, and effective communication on our happiness and well-being. By nurturing meaningful relationships, adopting a service-oriented mindset, and shifting our focus from ourselves to others, we enrich our lives and create a lasting positive influence on those around us. This chapter underscores that true happiness and fulfilment stem from our ability to build and maintain strong, empathetic, and supportive connections, both personally and professionally. By prioritising the needs of others and embracing a life of service, we cultivate a legacy of kindness, cooperation, and mutual respect that enhances not only our own lives but also the lives of those we touch.

KEY TAKEAWAYS

1. **Human Connection is Essential:** Relationships are fundamental to our well-being. Building and maintaining strong, supportive relationships requires intentionality, effort and empathy.

2. **Active Listening and Communication:** Effective communication is crucial in building and sustaining relationships. This involves active listening, empathetic engagement, and a balanced approach to expressing oneself.

3. **Conflict Resolution:** Addressing misunderstandings and disagreements promptly and respectfully helps maintain healthy relationships. Avoiding conflict can lead to resentment and weakened bonds.

4. **Mutual Support and Appreciation:** Offering and seeking support, expressing gratitude, and recognising others' contributions strengthen social bonds and enhance relationships.

5. **Altruism and Service Orientation:** Adopting a service-oriented mindset and living altruistically, without expecting reciprocation, fosters deeper connections and a sense of fulfilment.

6. **Shift Focus to Others:** Moving the centre of attention from ourselves to others leads to a more inclusive and cooperative environment, fostering mutual respect and collaboration.

7. **Balance in Giving:**   While generosity is essential, it must be balanced to avoid exploitation. Strategic giving ensures sustainable support without depleting personal resources.

8. **Legacy of Relationships:**   At the end of our lives, the quality and depth of our relationships matter more than our achievements. Building a life rich in meaningful connections is the true measure of a well-lived life.

By integrating these principles into our daily lives, we can create a more compassionate, connected and fulfilling existence, ultimately contributing to a more harmonious and supportive society.

CHAPTER 5

DEVELOPING DETACHMENT AND RESILIENCE

INTRODUCTION:

So far, in the previous chapters, we have explored the foundational elements of a fulfilling life. In Chapter 1, we discussed the importance of finding our flow, a sense of duty, and purpose. These elements guide our actions and set us on the path to achieving happiness. Chapter 2 highlighted why the ends don't justify the means and emphasised the necessity of developing the right attitude and mindset to become happy and successful. In Chapter 3, we examined certain detrimental practices that can derail our pursuit of happiness. Chapter 4 illustrated the significance of taking others along on our journey and living a life of service.

In this chapter, we will delve into a crucial aspect of maintaining happiness and well-being: resilience. No matter how content we are with our lives, we will inevitably face challenges that threaten to overwhelm us. These moments, which I refer to as the low points in life, are universal. Everyone encounters their own set of challenges, and it often feels like we bear the heaviest burdens. However, this perception is subjective. If we take a broader view, we realise that everyone has difficulties – they just might not be as visible or openly discussed.

Each person is the best judge of the challenges they face. What might seem manageable to one person could be overwhelming to another. This chapter is dedicated to understanding the importance of resilience and developing a sense of detachment that will help us navigate through our toughest times.

THIS TOO SHALL PASS

You may have heard an ancient Jewish folk tale that goes like this:

There was a king named Solomon who wanted to find a cure for depression. He gathered all his wise men and asked them, "Why don't you go out and find me a ring that will make sad people happy and happy people sad?"

The wise men set out to fulfil the king's request. They returned with a ring inscribed with the words, "This too shall pass."

When the king was enjoying himself and feeling very happy, his wise men presented him with the ring. The moment he looked at the inscription, all his happiness and enjoyment vanished. He realised that the fun he was having was temporary, which made him feel glum. However, when he looked at the ring again, he felt quite cheerful, knowing that this too shall pass.

King Solomon found that whenever he looked at the ring, his mood would immediately change. This story is a powerful example of developing resilience.

The most important lesson from this tale is that everything we face in life is temporary. When we die, we take nothing with us—neither fame nor our physical bodies. Therefore, we must understand that everything around us changes with time. We should strive to find as much happiness as possible during our time in this world.

As we face life's challenges, we must remember that in 10 years, when we look back and reflect on our past struggles, we will likely think, "Hey, that wasn't so difficult." In retrospect, we often see how overwhelmed we felt during the challenge and realise how much we have grown since then.

"Happiness is like those palaces in fairytales whose gates are guarded by dragons: We must fight to conquer it."
—Alexandre Dumas

And obviously, we can't travel back to the past and talk to ourselves, but we can use this wisdom in the future whenever we encounter challenges again. By understanding that everything in life is temporary, we can approach future difficulties with the knowledge that they too will pass. As the saying goes, "There is always light at the end of the tunnel." We will feel much better, just like King Solomon did when he looked at the ring and realised that his unhappiness was temporary.

The best way to address any situation is to focus on the present. The present is the only thing that is real. The past is just a memory, and the future is merely a story that our minds project. Therefore, we must start by accepting the present moment as it is.

Life may not always unfold as we envisioned it, but instead of getting caught up in analysing why things are the way they are, we should begin by acting in the present. As we engage with the present moment, our minds will naturally drift towards the future. The key is to gently bring our attention back to the here and now.

Have faith in the future. Ultimately, if we live each day fully and perfectly in the present moment, that will shape our future. By focusing on the present, we build a foundation for a fulfilling and resilient life.

This perspective helps us navigate life's ups and downs with a balanced mindset. Whenever we face hardships, we can remind ourselves that, like everything else, they are temporary and will pass. Similarly, in times of joy, we can cherish those moments, knowing they are fleeting. Embracing the impermanent nature of life allows us to appreciate the highs and endure the lows, ultimately fostering a deeper sense of resilience and contentment.

It also reminds me of a story from World War II. A captain leading his troop found themselves surrounded by the enemy, and there was a palpable sense of despair among the men because they knew there was no way to escape. The scout, tasked with monitoring the enemy, informed the captain of their dire situation.

In response, the captain gave an unexpected order: he instructed his men to make coffee. Bewildered, the soldiers wondered why their captain would ask them to make coffee when they were surrounded by the enemy. Despite their confusion, they followed his instructions and made the coffee.

As they sat and drank their coffee, the scout, who was closely observing the enemy's movements, approached the captain with new information. He had noticed a small break in the enemy's formation and suggested that, under the cover of darkness, they might be able to escape. Acting on this insight, the troop did exactly that and managed to escape.

This story illustrates a crucial lesson: the captain did not succumb to worry about the future or allow his men to become paralysed by fear. He understood that in their difficult situation, there was nothing immediate they could do, so he chose to keep his men calm and occupied. Their good fortune came from a relaxed state of mind, which allowed them to seize the opportunity when it presented itself.

Similarly, in our own lives, we may encounter challenges where no immediate solution is apparent. In such situations, it is often best to adopt a wait-and-watch strategy rather than becoming overwhelmed with worry. By settling down and clearing our minds, we create the mental space needed to either let the problem resolve itself or recognise a solution when it arises.

This approach teaches us that sometimes the best course of action is to remain calm and patient. Just as the captain's calm demeanour ultimately led to their escape, our composed mindset can help us navigate through our challenges more effectively. Whether by finding a sudden break in the situation or simply allowing time to provide clarity, staying grounded and patient can often lead to the best outcomes.

Another analogy that I would like to share to illustrate building resilience is as follows:

Imagine going to a lake and disturbing the water at the bottom. Soon enough, the mud will start clouding the water, making it difficult to see even your feet. The water, which was clear before, becomes so muddy that visibility is severely compromised. Similarly, when we let disturbances or challenging situations get the better of us, our thoughts become muddled, and we lose clarity.

The only way to regain clarity is to be patient and let the mud settle down. We need to have faith that the dust will settle, and soon enough, the water will be clear again, allowing us to see our feet. In the same way, if we remain calm and patient, we will eventually regain clarity and be able to handle the situation effectively.

While waiting for the dust to settle, we shouldn't waste our time. Instead, we should act on whatever we can do and trust that the dots will somehow connect. To use Steve Jobs' analogy, "You can only connect the dots looking backward." Therefore, we must follow our minds and intuition as we move forward.

Even though we may not understand why we are going through a difficult phase at the moment, we should have faith that, like the mud in the water, the situation will eventually clear up if we keep our minds calm. By maintaining a calm mindset, we gain the clarity needed to navigate through challenges.

In doing so, we enhance our maturity and resilience. Life's challenges often seem overwhelming when we are in the midst of them, but with patience and a calm approach, we can see them for what they are: temporary disturbances that will eventually pass. By keeping our minds steady, we can find solutions, make better decisions and, ultimately, grow stronger from the experience.

In conclusion, whether through the wisdom of "this too shall pass," the calmness of the WWII captain, or the clarity gained by letting the mud settle in a lake, these analogies teach us valuable lessons about resilience. By focusing on the present moment, remaining patient, and maintaining faith in our ability to overcome obstacles, we build a foundation for handling life's uncertainties with grace and strength.

"Happiness is contagious, pass it on."

—**Anonymous**

NETWORK OF WELL-WISHERS

Research shows that very loving parents, who give unconditional love to their children and provide for their basic needs – such as food, clothing, and shelter – create a conducive environment for their development. These children tend to grow up to be more resilient and more comfortable with life. This insight underscores the importance of cultivating a network of well-wishers and supportive friends in our quest to become more resilient and happy, as well as to guard against potential challenges in life.

Often, as we get married and have children, we become so busy that we neglect our friendships and fail to invest in building and nurturing relationships. This is something we must avoid because when times get tough and we need support, there might not be anyone there to help us if we haven't maintained our connections.

Therefore, we should make it a priority to set aside time every week to call our old friends and nurture those relationships. We should also develop the habit of not saying no to helping others. We are never too busy if someone asks for our help, especially our friends. Reminding ourselves, "We are never too busy to help them," reinforces the importance of being there for others.

Helping others is the best way to pay it forward. We should go out of our way to assist those who are truly in need. This altruistic approach helps us cultivate and nurture relationships that will protect and support us during rough or difficult times in our own lives.

As we engage in acts of kindness, it is crucial to do so from the bottom of our hearts, without expecting anything in return. Our actions should not feel forced or transactional. By genuinely helping others unconditionally, we foster a community of support and goodwill. Constantly seeking opportunities to assist others strengthens our bonds and enriches our lives.

In conclusion, building resilience involves not only personal strategies but also creating and maintaining a supportive network. By investing in relationships, offering unconditional help, and fostering a community of mutual support, we enhance our ability to face life's challenges with strength and grace.

Another way to cultivate a good set of well-wishers is to engage in activities you enjoy and connect with people who share similar interests. For example, if you enjoy playing chess, you might join a chess club that meets on weekends and build a network of friends there. Similarly, if you enjoy running, you could join a group of people who also love to run and create a network of like-minded individuals.

Having such networks has been shown to provide comfort, a sense of belonging, and a feeling of community, all of which contribute to happiness. Additionally, these networks ensure that when you go through difficult times, there are people who care about you and are ready to support you.

> *"There is no happiness like that of being loved by your fellow beings and feeling that your presence is an addition to their comfort."*
>
> —**Charlotte Brontë**

NOT LET THE SITUATION GET THE BETTER OF US

In our world, we face 2 types of situations: those within our control and those outside of our control. However, if we take a holistic view, we often find that situations we perceive as beyond our control might actually be within our reach. Sometimes, we simply lack the skills or creativity to bring them into our circle of influence.

Consider this classic example: As a team manager, you may frequently encounter complaints about another team from your own team members. When asked about their progress, they might blame the other team for not pulling their weight, hindering their own performance. The key point here is that, even if they depend on another team, it is a skill to ensure collaboration and complementary performance.

Effective collaboration is a skill that needs to be developed and nurtured.

Now, let's turn to situations within our control. In any situation we face, it's not the situation itself that's under our control, but our response to it. Recognising this distinction is crucial so that we are not overwhelmed by the situation. We will inevitably face many unanticipated challenges, which might make us feel angry with ourselves, others, or even God, wondering why we are in this situation while others seem happy.

It's important to understand that the situation itself is not within our control. Everyone experiences their share of good and bad situations. What we can control is our response and reaction to these situations. The best strategy when facing a difficult and inexplicable situation is to avoid dissipating our energy by asking, "Why am I in this situation?"

When we visit a doctor, the doctor listens to our symptoms and, based on those symptoms or test results, advises on the next steps for a cure. The doctor does not waste time questioning why the situation has arisen but focuses on what needs to be done to resolve it. Similarly, in life, we should not waste our energy constantly asking "why" because there often isn't a single reason for a situation. The world is complex, with interrelated systems, making it impossible to pinpoint one cause. Situations arise from a combination of factors.

Therefore, we should not dissipate our energy on questioning, but instead focus on taking action.

The strategy I have found very useful is to shift focus from the challenge or situation to taking action. When we face challenges, much of our energy is wasted trying to understand why the situation has arisen. This often leads to a negative cycle of blaming others for the situation and their lack of responsibility. We tend to blame everyone but ourselves, though we shouldn't blame ourselves either. Instead, we should accept the situation as it is and focus on taking action. We should strive to be proactive rather than seeing the situation as a threat.

First, when facing any situation, we should gather all the facts. Often, our emotions cloud our judgement, preventing us from seeing the situation clearly. By gathering facts, we can look at the situation objectively, much like a doctor who prescribes tests and analyses the results. This approach is far more effective than dwelling on why the situation occurred or berating ourselves for being in it. Complaining about the environment that led to the problem is also futile. Like a doctor, we should focus on gathering facts.

Secondly, we need to break the situation into manageable components. Dealing with smaller, separate parts makes the overall challenge more approachable.

Thirdly, we should seek different perspectives, especially if the situation is complex. Just as doctors consult colleagues for new ideas and insights about difficult cases, we should seek outside opinions to gain a fresh perspective on our challenges. This approach can be particularly useful for complex business problems, allowing us to stay objective and find effective solutions.

Fourth, it is helpful to classify the situation as either within our control or beyond it. If certain aspects are out of our control, we need to make peace with them and move on, focusing our energy on the things we can control. Our minds generate approximately 60,000 thoughts a day, many of which dissipate our energy on uncontrollable factors.

Why not focus all our energy on what we can control and take appropriate action? By doing this, we can take charge of the situation instead of letting it overwhelm us. We should stay focused on our course of action, seek iterative opinions, continuously review the facts and try different approaches. Maintaining optimism and faith that things will eventually fall into place will help us address the situation effectively.

> *"Happy people plan actions, they don't plan results."*
> —**Dennis Waitley**

ACHIEVING MASTERY

When we are going through a rough patch in life and feeling miserable, we sometimes start doubting our capability and ability to perform. These rough patches could be due to factors completely out of our control. Whatever the cause, having some consistency in our lives can be very helpful.

A valuable principle to adopt is to achieve mastery in certain areas of our life. This allows us to look in the mirror and confidently affirm that we are among the best in those areas. Even if we excel in just one area, it is sufficient; it is not necessary to excel in all areas.

To illustrate, let us consider some popular athletes, such as the famous basketball player Michael Jordan. At the peak of his career, he was the best basketball player, and no one could question his skills. He faced some very tough times, such as the death of his father and numerous complaints about his gambling habits. Despite these challenges, Michael Jordan emerged strong because he knew he excelled in one area—basketball. No matter the challenge, he believed he could overcome it.

Similarly, even if we cannot be like Michael Jordan in basketball, we can achieve a similar level of excellence in whatever field aligns with our interests and confidence. As we strive for world-class excellence in a specific area, we will develop the courage and fortitude to be resilient in other areas where we face challenges.

For example, it is well-known that when people go through personal tragedy, they often immerse themselves in their work. This helps them take their mind off the tragedy they have suffered. Hence, this is a perfectly legitimate strategy to adopt.

We must also realise that we cannot contribute equally to all things. When we judge others, we do so based on our own beliefs and definitions of success, which may be very different from what the other person values. Similarly, when others judge us, many may not like the way we look or behave. We will always have admirers, as well as critics.

The only way to stay positive and not be influenced by negativity is to do what we love and commit to it fully until we achieve world-class excellence. Achieving mastery should be in an area that aligns with our strengths. Many people try to work on their weaknesses, but this is often very difficult. Overcoming years of conditioning and genetic predispositions to turn a weakness into a strength is challenging. Therefore, it is more effective to focus on our strengths.

When striving for mastery, it is crucial to align our efforts with our core strengths. As we become proficient in one area, we will realise that our performance in other areas becomes less significant.

I remember a story my uncle told me long ago. He was on a flight and met a very famous actor of that time. My uncle could hardly recognise him. He wasn't embarrassed to share this story because he was a businessman and very good at what he did. He didn't care whether he knew all the film actors or not and had no interest in keeping up with the film industry.

Similarly, we need to understand that we may only know a few things, but we should know them so well that we achieve world-class mastery in that area. Warren Buffet once said that he sticks within his circle of competence. This is why he doesn't regret not investing in technology firms, as he freely admits he doesn't understand them. By sticking to his circle of competence, Warren Buffet has become one of the richest men in the investing world and has achieved extraordinary success.

By achieving mastery, we gain significant confidence that helps us withstand negativity and develop resilience to overcome personal setbacks and challenges in life.

OUR REACTION FRAMEWORK TO SITUATIONS

One important aspect I want to highlight is how we react to situations that occur in our lives. Our methodology for responding can be fine-tuned to build our resilience.

For example, when faced with a challenge, do we believe that it was entirely caused by external factors, or do we recognise that we may have contributed to the problem and therefore take responsibility for fixing it?

There's a beautiful saying: "Whatever happens, happens for the best." If we adopt this attitude and see every problem as having a positive aspect, we will feel less helpless. We will start taking responsibility for the problem and take action to resolve it.

The second question to consider is: do we believe that the situation was caused by various factors, and can the root cause be influenced, or is it entirely out of our control? Developing an attitude that acknowledges the situation and the factors contributing to it, and deciding to take action, can make us feel less helpless and more resilient.

The third variable to consider is: do we believe that the situation will lead to more problems, creating an avalanche effect? Or do we have a habit of making a mountain out of a molehill? Alternatively, do we believe that we can control the situation and take action to ensure it is managed?

By adopting these perspectives, we can better manage our reactions to situations and build our resilience.

So, as you can see, our reaction to a situation should follow a three-part framework. The first part is to take responsibility for the situation. Acknowledge how we may have contributed to it and identify what we can do to correct it.

Secondly, while some root causes might be beyond our control, we need to believe that we can influence and change them to bring the situation under control quickly.

Lastly, we must avoid catastrophising. Always consider a situation to be something manageable and not let it overwhelm us. The overall framework emphasises not feeling helpless, taking responsibility, and taking control of our lives. By maintaining a positive attitude, we can face and address any situation that comes our way, improving it in the process.

Let us consider a simple example. Suppose we are diagnosed with a life-threatening disease. What would be our reaction? Are we going to say, "This is not my fault; it's due to genetics," and subsequently blame our forefathers or parents for passing down the wrong genetic material? Or are we going to say, "I have this genetic disease, but I am going to seek help. I will look for possible remedies, like developing a better lifestyle and exercise regime. I am going to take control of my life. And even if I have a terminal illness, I will ensure that whatever time I have left, I will spread happiness and make the situation better for myself and others."

By adopting this proactive and positive attitude, we can better manage and improve our circumstances, no matter how challenging they may be.

Thus, our reaction to a situation is crucial. We should not let the situation get the better of us or overwhelm us. By developing a framework that emphasises our ability to maintain control in a positive manner, we can navigate through challenges more effectively.

It's about maintaining a balanced perspective. For example, if we lose a job, do we allow ourselves to be consumed by despair, or do we look at it as an opportunity to explore new paths, acquire new skills, or pursue a passion? By focusing on what we can control and taking proactive steps, we foster resilience.

In essence, our reaction framework is about acknowledging our role in the situation, understanding what we can influence and maintaining a positive outlook that encourages action and responsibility. This approach not only helps us handle immediate challenges but also strengthens our overall resilience for future difficulties.

> *"Happiness comes from living as you need to, as you*
> *want to. As your inner voice tells you to.*
> *Happiness comes from being who you are, instead*
> *of who you think you are supposed to be."*
> —Shonda Rhimes

DEALING WITH STRESS

One of the most important skills we need to develop is our ability to handle stressful situations. In our fast-paced and competitive world, stressful situations are inevitable. Some of these situations might be anticipated, while others are completely unforeseen and beyond our control.

So, how do we handle stress? Stress can have very negative psychological and physiological consequences. It can lead to various ailments and diseases, exacerbated by today's work environment and heightened stress levels. To build resilience, we must understand what causes our stress and identify the trigger points that help us manage it effectively.

When we analyse a stressful situation, we realise that the situation itself is not to blame. Stress arises from our lack of skill in handling it and our tendency to let it overwhelm us. Therefore, the first step is to recognise that the stressfulness of a situation is a reflection of our ability to manage it.

Consider people in our personal lives who handle stressful situations calmly and with a plan, without becoming perturbed or overwhelmed. This demonstrates that it is not the situation itself, but our response to it, that determines the level of stress we experience.

To improve our ability to manage stress, we can adopt the following strategies:

Identify Stress Triggers: Recognise the specific factors that cause stress. Understanding these triggers can help us prepare and respond more effectively.

Develop Coping Mechanisms: Create a set of strategies for dealing with stress, such as deep breathing exercises, mindfulness, or taking breaks when needed.

Stay Organised: Keeping a well-organised schedule and maintaining a tidy environment can reduce the chaos that often contributes to stress.

Seek Support: Don't hesitate to reach out for help from friends, family, or professionals. Sharing our concerns can provide relief and new perspectives on managing stress.

Focus on Solutions: Instead of dwelling on the problems, shift your focus to finding solutions. This proactive approach can reduce feelings of helplessness.

Maintain a Healthy Lifestyle: Regular exercise, a balanced diet and adequate sleep are crucial in managing stress levels and overall well-being.

By adopting these strategies and continuously working on our stress management skills, we can handle stressful situations more effectively and maintain our resilience in the face of challenges.

The difference between peak athletes and those who are not as successful, despite having similar skill sets, often lies in their ability to handle stress rather than their inherent talents. Two equally competent athletes can perform very differently on the world stage because of how they manage stress constructively.

Peak athletes have mastered the art of stress management. They understand that high-pressure situations are part of their journey and have developed strategies to cope with them. This ability to stay calm and focused under pressure allows them to perform at their best when it matters most.

On the other hand, athletes who struggle with stress may find their performance hindered, despite their high skill levels. Stress can cause them to overthink, lose focus, and make errors that they would not typically make in a more relaxed environment. The pressure can overwhelm them, leading to subpar performances.

Thinking handicaps people typically encounter when dealing with stressful situations.

The first thinking handicap is generalising the situation and, as the saying goes, "making a mountain out of a molehill."

We need to recognise this pattern of generalisation when faced with a difficult situation. In this mindset, we feel as though the entire roof is going to crash down on us, and everything good in our life is about to end. This kind of catastrophising is very unhealthy and immediately impairs our ability to handle the situation objectively.

The second type of thinking that causes stress is being overly logical or over-analysing the situation. As the saying goes, "Analysis leads to paralysis." This is especially true for people who are very logical in their thinking. They tend to interlink and intertwine seemingly unrelated events from the past with the current situation, ultimately creating additional stress for themselves and their teams by planning for highly unlikely scenarios. This over-analysis is another pattern of thinking we need to be aware of, as it significantly increases our stress levels.

Another cause of stress is the presence of random thoughts that continuously intrude our minds. These thoughts may not be correlated, yet we start seeing connections where none exist. This leads to the shutting down of our logical brain because the structure of our brain is such that the hippocampus and amygdala control the neural circuit trail before any impulse reaches the neocortex, or logical brain. Essentially, if our reptilian brain takes control of our thinking, we lose our capacity to think logically and address the situation at hand.

When this happens, our thoughts take over, looping like a broken tape recorder, repeatedly fixating on what is bothering us. This constant mental repetition clouds our ability to think of solutions or gain a sense of perspective about the situation at hand.

To manage stress effectively, it is crucial to be aware of these thinking patterns and take steps to counteract them. Practising mindfulness, focusing on the present moment, and developing a positive and proactive attitude can help us break free from these mental traps. By doing so, we can enhance our ability to handle stress constructively and maintain our resilience in the face of challenges.

Let us now examine what is causing this stress.

The first trigger, I would argue, is ambiguity. When we encounter a situation that is new or unfamiliar to us, we are often unsure of what to do next. This is especially true in today's business environment, where managers and leaders must navigate scenarios for which they have neither training nor prior experience. So, how do we deal with such ambiguous situations?

The second cause of personal stress is our significant attachment to objects or relationships, leading us to dwell on worst-case scenarios. For instance, when our children are out and haven't returned on time, our strong attachment to them can cause us to imagine highly unlikely negative outcomes.

Therefore, this attachment to objects or relationships heightens stress levels. An example of this is road rage: if you are fond of your car and someone bumps into it at a traffic signal, you may become very upset and stressed. Excessive attachment to objects needs to be controlled.

We must moderate our attachment to things to ensure it doesn't hinder our happiness. The best way to overcome this is to remind ourselves that our ultimate goal is happiness and that objects and relationships are temporary. They exist today but might not be there tomorrow. We need to understand that we will not always have the objects we are passionate about or highly attached to.

A very simple example is when we were kids and were very attached to our toys. If someone took a toy away from a child, they would immediately start crying. Even if the child had only owned the toy for a few hours, they would become very attached to it. In hindsight, this attachment seems amusing because we have outgrown it and matured.

Now, consider cars, power, and wealth as toys for grown-ups. By understanding their true worth, we can see how our increased attachment to these material things and relationships elevates our stress levels, robbing us of happiness and a good night's rest.

Stress can also stem from our positions. Excessive attachment to our job, title, and status causes so much stress that we begin to lose our happiness. For example, receiving a bad review can wipe the smile off our faces. This shouldn't be the case. While it's true that we work hard and hold important titles, we should remind ourselves that we are doing a great job and not become too attached to these titles.

We should tell ourselves that perhaps tomorrow, we will find an even better job or receive a much better title. This mindset helps us manage our stress and maintain our happiness, regardless of our current position or status.

We should not overly stress about what we have today because everything is temporary. Better prospects await, and the future will likely be brighter than the present. Even if it gets worse, that's alright, because we may learn valuable lessons along the way.

Another significant source of stress is engaging in activities that we inherently dislike or that are not aligned with our culture or value system. Persisting in such activities only increases our stress.

A good example is being stuck in a job and environment where you cannot bond with your peers because their values are vastly different from yours. In such situations, the best strategy is to move on. Feeling like a fish out of water not only leads to stress but also undermines our happiness.

The best way I've found to handle stressful situations is to develop a process or system that we can rely on and mentally rehearse to prepare for such scenarios. Another effective way to manage stress is to ask for help. Sometimes, we face situations that are difficult to understand and manage on our own. It is perfectly okay to ask for help. Asking for help is not a sign of weakness. We can confide in trusted individuals and seek their assistance.

We can ask them, "Are we looking at the situation from the right perspective?" Often, when you discuss the issue with someone you trust, solutions begin to emerge. Sometimes, individually, we lack the knowledge or perspective to address the problem effectively.

We should not blame ourselves for being unable to think outside the box due to stress. Seeking different viewpoints from others can provide relief from the problem and help us navigate stressful situations more effectively.

Another effective way to manage stress is to avoid asking ourselves, "Why has this particular situation arisen?" As I mentioned earlier, many situations are beyond our control. We are bound to encounter our share of stressful circumstances in life that we cannot change. Rather than wasting time and energy asking, "Why me?" and "Why am I facing this situation?" it is much more productive to ask, "What?"

By shifting from 'why' to 'what', we can ask, "What should I do, given that this situation has arisen?" This shift in focus helps us improve our logical thinking and develop creative solutions to face and manage the situation.

Embracing this mindset allows us to take proactive steps, rather than dwelling on the uncontrollable aspects of life. By focusing on actionable solutions, we empower ourselves to handle stress more effectively and maintain a positive outlook despite the challenges we face.

> *"Happiness is letting go of what you think*
> *your life is supposed to look like and celebrating*
> *it for everything that it is."*
>
> **—Mandy Hale**

SELF-AWARENESS AND SELF-CONTROL

To build resilience and effectively handle life's challenges, it's essential to develop self-awareness and improve our self-control.

There are 2 key traits often observed in people with low self-awareness. First, they lack clarity about what they want from their lives. Second, they lack self-control.

When we look at successful individuals, whether it is Mahatma Gandhi, Nelson Mandela, or others, a common quality among them is clear: they are very clear about their mission and values in life.

Therefore, it is crucial for us to cultivate a sense of clarity and purpose. This doesn't necessarily happen overnight. We can always be in search of our life's meaning, but we should always have a sense of direction and goals at any given time and commit ourselves to them. Discovering our purpose is a journey, and it's okay to change our direction as we grow and learn more about ourselves. Rather than claiming to have found our purpose on day one, we should keep the question open and continue seeking clarity.

Without clarity, we are like a ship without a rudder, drifting aimlessly wherever the wind blows. This leads to an unfulfilling life, often lived to please others, under the guise of love or loyalty.

We must develop a clear sense of purpose to live our lives in a way that brings us happiness and fulfilment. We don't need to justify this to anyone, nor should we seek others' approval for our life's purpose. Self-awareness means having clarity about our life's purpose and direction.

> *"To succeed in your mission, you must have single-minded devotion to your goal."*
> —Dr. A.P.J. Abdul Kalam

People who lack this clarity constantly seek direction from others and bend to external influences, lacking the resolve to stand up for what they believe because they don't know what they truly want in life.

Another extreme example of an incorrect position is being very clear about what one wants but not willing to take others along. This also indicates a lack of self-awareness in terms of understanding how we present ourselves to the world. While having clarity is crucial, it is equally important that others understand and align with our purpose. Without this shared understanding, we won't achieve our goals or lead a fulfilling life.

For instance, consider Mahatma Gandhi, the Father of our nation. He had a clear vision of what he wanted to achieve and was an excellent communicator who could effectively convey his ideas to others. Similarly, Dr. Martin Luther King Jr. was a remarkable communicator with a clear message, inspiring many to join his cause.

Thus, it is vital not only to have personal clarity, but also to bring others along on our journey. By doing so, we build trustful relationships and strong friendships, which further help us discover ourselves and refine our path towards achieving our sense of purpose in life.

However, many deterrents or challenges can arise on our road to self-discovery, and one of the biggest hindrances is our ego. When we hold powerful positions or have significant experience, we might develop a sense of entitlement, which hinders our communication with others and openness to feedback. This erosion of our ability to be self-aware and understand how we come across to others can be detrimental.

Experience and power often bring overconfidence, leading us to stop questioning our assumptions. This situation is akin to adjusting the focus on binoculars or a camera lens to see an object clearly. Sometimes, changing the lens is necessary, much like how photographers understand the need for different perspectives.

Similarly, by valuing others' opinions, inviting criticism, and maintaining humility, we gain clarity about ourselves, the world, and how others perceive us. This process of continuous learning and openness fosters strong relationships which are critical to achieving our goals.

So, the second part of self-awareness is self-control. Many times, I have seen very successful people lose their self-control in meetings or during highly stressful situations. While it is natural to be under stress, it does not justify taking out anger on subordinates, family members, or children.

Such behaviour creates a negative spiral, leading to alienation and deteriorating relationships. As these relationships erode, focus on work diminishes, perpetuating a further decline into negativity.

The key to self-control lies in awareness of our reactions when faced with challenging situations. For example, when someone speaks rudely to us without any fault of ours, the immediate reaction might be to retaliate angrily. However, it is more beneficial to pause and reflect on why the other person is behaving this way.

Some might view this self-analysis as unnecessary, but it is not for the other person's benefit—it is an exercise in self-restraint and maintaining control, regardless of the situation. Just as we go to the gym to exercise our muscles and improve our appearance, we should view life's situations as exercises for our brain, building our ability to practice self-control. Like any other skill, the more we practice, the better we become.

People with strong self-control lead happier and more fulfilling lives because they are less disturbed by adverse situations. It is easy to find peace while on vacation or when alone, but we must remember that we cannot live in isolation. We need people and must engage fully with the various experiences life presents, both favourable and unfavourable.

Therefore, we need self-control to avoid immediate, reactive responses to challenging situations. Instead, we should let the situation absorb, be aware of it, and exercise good judgement to create a better response. The best way to practice self-control is to have a clear vision and a powerful mission statement that guides our life. When we focus on a larger vision, minor disturbances do not affect us mentally or emotionally, allowing us to operate at our logical best and be our best selves.

> *"Most people would rather be certain they're miserable than risk being happy."*
> —Dr Robert Anthony

A very good example of self-awareness and self-control is when we are at a train station with many trains passing by. As we sit there, we do not immediately jump onto any train, do we?!

Similarly, why should we let ourselves plunge into any problem and challenges that come our way?

A sense of direction and purpose helps us recognise the right train that will take us to our desired destination. Once we achieve this clarity, we can confidently catch the right train. This careful consideration and deliberate action are at the heart of self-awareness.

So, next time, pause and observe, identifying which train we want to board, and go for it!

> *"Happiness cannot be traveled to, owned, earned, worn, or consumed. Happiness is the spiritual experience of living every minute with love, grace, and gratitude."*
> —Denis Waitley

CONCLUSION

In this chapter, we have delved into the vital aspects of resilience, emphasising that life's challenges are inevitable but temporary. By adopting a perspective of impermanence, as highlighted in the story of King Solomon's ring, we can navigate hardships with a balanced mindset. We explored the significance of maintaining calm in crises, as illustrated by the WWII captain's unexpected decision to make coffee, and the analogy of letting muddy water settle to regain clarity. Additionally, we discussed the importance of building a network of well-wishers, not letting situations overwhelm us, achieving mastery, and developing a structured reaction framework. We also examined how self-awareness and self-control are essential for resilience and handling stress effectively.

KEY TAKEAWAYS

1. **Impermanence and Perspective:** Recognising that all situations, whether good or bad, are temporary, helps us maintain balance and resilience.
2. **Calmness in Crisis:** Staying calm and patient, even in difficult situations, can lead to better outcomes and clearer thinking.
3. **Building a Support Network:** Maintaining and nurturing relationships provides emotional support during tough times and fosters resilience.
4. **Proactive Response:** Focusing on actionable solutions, rather than dwelling on uncontrollable factors, helps us take control of our lives.
5. **Mastery and Confidence:** Achieving excellence in a specific area boosts confidence and helps us tackle other challenges more effectively.

6. **Self-Awareness and Self-Control:** Developing clarity about our goals and practising self-control enables us to respond to situations thoughtfully rather than reactively.

7. **Stress Management:** Identifying stress triggers, developing coping mechanisms, and maintaining a healthy lifestyle are crucial for managing stress and building resilience.

8. **Positive Attitude:** Adopting a positive outlook and believing that every challenge has a solution fosters resilience and helps us navigate life's ups and downs.

9. **Continuous Improvement:** Viewing life's challenges as exercises for growth and continuously seeking to improve our responses, helps us build a resilient mindset.

Ultimately, embracing these principles helps us live a more fulfilling and resilient life, capable of weathering any storm with grace and strength.

CHAPTER 6

FINDING BALANCE AND PEACE

INTRODUCTION:

So far in this book, we have explored various dimensions of building happiness. We began by discussing how to find moments of flow and purpose in life and the importance of focusing on our duties. In the second chapter, we emphasised that the ends do not justify the means. Developing the right attitude and mindset is critical for dealing with life's challenges, helping us stay happy on our journey while achieving our mission and goals.

In chapter 3, we examined the need to avoid certain inherent practices that can derail our happiness. These practices might seem natural but can lead us astray if not managed properly. We must find ways to handle such situations and avoid traps that undermine our fulfilment.

Chapter 4 highlighted the importance of taking others along on our journey. Life must be lived with the support of others, as our relationships and bonds with people ensure that our journey and quest to achieve our goals are both fulfilling and satisfying.

In chapter 5, we discussed the importance of developing resilience. Resilience acts as a protective layer that helps us navigate significant setbacks, whether professional or personal, with grace and composure.

This brings us to the current chapter, where we will talk about finding balance and inner peace. Achieving this balance will give us a sense of fulfilment and allow us to experience joy and happiness, regardless of the situations we face. We will delve deeper into how to maintain equanimity and poise, no matter where we are in life or what goals we have achieved.

The essence of this chapter is understanding "how to have a true sense of assurance and balance as we pursue our higher goals and live our purpose in life."

> **"Saying yes to happiness means learning to say no to the things and people that stress you out."**
> —**Thema Davis**

WHAT IS UNHAPPINESS?

In our quest to find balance and inner peace, let us start by asking: "What is unhappiness?" When we say we are unhappy, what does that truly mean? One of the fundamental realisations is that unhappiness is not real. It is just our mind telling us a story, and we have started believing in that story.

If we delve deeper, we will also realise that any form of unhappiness has its roots in some kind of attachment. For instance, if you observe young children, you will rarely see them groaning, worried, or unhappy in any situation. Even children who have significant illnesses or are born with challenges are often very happy. It is their parents who are worried and unhappy, not the child.

"Why is the child so happy despite the hardship and challenges?" The parents understand the gravity of the situation, but the child does not. This clearly shows that the child can be happy despite the problems because the child is not attached to anything in life, unlike adults who are attached to various things.

As adults, we might be attached to our titles at work, the power we hold due to our positions, our family members, our near and dear ones, or our friends. We might also be attached to our sense of self or ego. Whatever the attachment is, whether it is material or relational, it is often the main source of our unhappiness. The only way to find peace and joy in our life is to let go of these attachments.

Now, this is easier said than done. But one way to contemplate our attachments is to think about our death. It is common knowledge that when we die, we cannot take anything with us. This thought can help us realise the transient nature of our attachments and the futility of clinging to them.

Reflecting on our mortality can give us perspective. It reminds us that our attachments are temporary and that true peace and happiness come from within, not from external possessions or relationships. By understanding and gradually letting go of our attachments, we can start to cultivate a deeper sense of inner peace and balance in our lives.

This journey towards inner peace involves mindfulness and self-awareness. It requires us to observe our thoughts and emotions without judgement, to understand the stories our mind creates, and to gently release the hold these stories have on us. As we practice this, we will find that our sense of well-being becomes less dependent on external circumstances and more rooted in our inner state of mind.

In this chapter, we will explore practical steps and strategies to help us detach from our attachments and cultivate a state of equanimity. We will learn how to navigate life's challenges with grace and poise and how to maintain a sense of joy and fulfilment regardless of the situations we face. By the end of this chapter, you will have a deeper understanding of how to achieve true balance and inner peace, living a life that is not only successful but also deeply satisfying.

This realisation should prompt us to ask ourselves: "Why are we attached to anything? Why are we attached to our wealth, our titles, when we cannot take anything with us when we die?" When we cling to attachments, we make our lives more sorrowful than necessary. It's easy to say we shouldn't be attached, but in practice, we often find ourselves still holding on.

The moment you read this, or if you've read similar messages in spiritual texts, you might feel inspired to practice detachment but find it challenging to do so. Situations start to control us, and our minds convince us that detachment is impossible, and attachment is necessary. However, if we consider that we cannot take anything from this world with us, it becomes clear that attachment is pointless.

Attachment sacrifices our happiness for something transient. We must understand that nothing is more important in life than happiness. Living a successful life means being truly happy.

If we are attached to material things and relationships, we won't find happiness, even if we attain the best of relationships, titles, money, and fame. The more we cling to these "toys," the more anxious and stressed we become, constantly trying to maintain certain positions and meet others' expectations. This doesn't mean we shouldn't live our lives fully. Some argue that attachment motivates achievement, but this isn't true.

It's not the goal that motivates people to achieve greatness, but the journey. Living a balanced and happy life leads to ultimate success. Consider 2 people studying for an exam. One is focused on becoming a gold medallist, leading to unnecessary stress that derails their present happiness. The other person also aspires to be a gold medallist but doesn't let this goal stress them out. They enjoy studying and learning. Without the stress, they perform their best.

We know that the second person is more likely to achieve the gold medal. Speaking from experience, I was a gold medallist in both my MBA and Engineering degrees, but I never felt stressed. Even though I wanted to be a gold medallist, I didn't think about it every day. Constantly thinking about it would have caused unnecessary stress and made me live in the future, worrying and compromising the present.

This lack of attachment is crucial for finding balance and peace. By focusing on the journey and enjoying each moment, we can achieve our goals without sacrificing our happiness. Detachment doesn't mean we lack ambition or drive; it means we live fully in the present, free from the anxiety and stress that come from clinging to outcomes. By practising detachment, we cultivate inner peace and balance, allowing us to live a truly fulfilling life.

> *"Doing what you like is freedom.*
> *Liking what you do is happiness."*
> —**Anonymous**

START SAYING YES TO LIFE

One of the most important practices that will help us find balance and peace in life is to start saying yes more often. Often, we fear that saying yes might derail us from our path, and we should be cautious about the choices we make and learn how to say no. However, from my personal experience, resistance to the new often leads to missed opportunities and experiences.

We frequently say no to people, situations, and new experiences. Many times, by saying no to others, we are inadvertently saying no to ourselves. When we have an interest or a passion, we often say no to pursuing it because we lack the courage and confidence to open up. This leads our minds to believe that we are not meant to pursue our passions, that it is not the right time, or that we need more preparation.

This mindset is detrimental to finding balance and peace. Life's situations can be good or bad, but we must accept that there is no such thing as a perfect situation. By embracing whatever comes our way, we allow ourselves to grow, learn and experience life fully.

Saying yes opens doors to new opportunities and experiences that enrich our lives. It helps us develop resilience and adaptability, key components of inner peace and balance. When we say yes, we step out of our comfort zones and embrace the unknown, which can be a powerful catalyst for personal growth.

Embracing this practice doesn't mean we abandon discernment or become overwhelmed by commitments. Instead, it means adopting a more open and receptive attitude toward life's possibilities. By doing so, we invite new experiences and perspectives that contribute to our overall well-being.

This approach also fosters a sense of gratitude and appreciation for life. When we say yes to new experiences, we learn to value and cherish each moment, finding joy in the journey rather than fixating on specific outcomes. This shift in perspective helps us maintain a sense of balance and inner peace, regardless of external circumstances.

Also, there is no such thing as an ideal situation. When we say 'no' to an opportunity, especially one we are passionate about, we deny ourselves the pleasure and growth that comes with it. For instance, if our company or boss extends an opportunity to us, or if a friend reaches out for help, and we say 'no' because we are uncertain if it aligns with our goals, we are merely being resistant to stepping out of our comfort zone. However, we should remember that even the best ideas and most successful ventures often have humble beginnings and their share of failures.

> *"Happiness will never come to those who don't appreciate what they already have."*
>
> —**Anonymous**

When we say 'no' to either ourselves or others, we find ourselves in a vicious circle of denying opportunities, ultimately not paying attention to new possibilities that arise. This can be catastrophic.

There are numerous business examples where large companies went bankrupt because they kept saying no, despite the world moving in a particular direction. A notable example is Blockbuster, once a top rental service for movies. Even though Netflix was an obvious competitor, Blockbuster did not recognise the threat. They continued to say 'no' to adapting to the new trend of online streaming, which allowed Netflix to take over the market, establish its leadership, and ultimately dominate. As a result, Blockbuster, a huge company, went bankrupt.

This downfall occurred because Blockbuster stopped saying 'yes' to new realities. They diluted their potential despite concrete evidence that the market was shifting towards online consumption. Many other successful companies have faced similar fates because they kept saying 'no' to changing market dynamics.

A similar principle applies to us. The world is constantly changing, and we need to be always on the lookout for new opportunities and experiences.

Saying 'yes' to new experiences doesn't mean blindly accepting every opportunity without discernment. Instead, it means being open and receptive to possibilities, even if they challenge us or push us out of our comfort zones. This openness can lead to personal and professional growth, resilience, and adaptability. It fosters a mindset of exploration and learning, which is essential in an ever-changing world.

Moreover, by saying 'yes', we cultivate a sense of gratitude and appreciation for what we have and the opportunities that come our way. This attitude helps us remain positive and proactive, contributing to our overall happiness and well-being. It encourages us to embrace life's unpredictability, turning potential challenges into valuable experiences.

And the best way to do that is to start saying 'Yes' and stop saying 'No'. Another negative consequence of saying 'No' is that it can isolate us. Often, friends reach out seeking our help to navigate unfamiliar situations. By saying 'No', we not only deny them assistance but also lose the opportunity to receive their support in the future when we might need it. This isolation can lead others to perceive us as rigid and unhelpful. To avoid this, we should remain open to saying 'Yes' to people and new ideas because the future is unpredictable.

We should follow our intuition like Steve Jobs, who famously told students that, "We can connect the dots only by looking backward." As long as we have a general sense of direction, we should be open to experimenting and trying new things. Professor Clayton Christensen explains this concept well in his strategic discourse, highlighting the importance of both deliberate and emergent strategies.

Deliberate strategy arises from conscious, thoughtful planning by leadership. This aligns with our discussion in Chapter 1, where we emphasised the importance of having a clear goal in life and focusing passionately on it. While it's crucial to maintain a deliberate strategy, as Christensen notes, we must also stay receptive to emergent strategies—those that arise from unplanned actions and changes in the market.

Like what Blockbuster faced when competition from Netflix emerged, completely disrupting the industry. The best way to balance, as Professor Clayton Christensen explains, is to assess the situation and ask ourselves, "Are we faced with a dynamic situation where things are changing rapidly?" This is especially crucial when running a business, particularly during the startup phase when revenue has not yet started flowing or the revenue model is still unproven.

We must remain continuously open to new ideas and experiences. Similarly, in our personal lives, when starting our careers, we should be receptive to new inputs and opportunities.

However, we should also maintain an overall deliberate strategy. Once we see progress in a particular area—say, we have matured our business and certain products are performing well, becoming the 'cash cows' of the business—we need to hit the accelerator and scale up.

At this stage, our focus on a deliberate strategy will yield much richer dividends. By balancing both deliberate and emergent strategies, we can navigate uncertainties and capitalise on opportunities. This approach not only applies to business but also to personal growth and development. Embracing change and staying flexible, while having a clear direction, ensures that we can adapt and thrive in an ever-evolving environment.

Applying this philosophy to a personal context, it is important to have a deliberate strategy. For example, if we are currently employed or doing well in business or as professionals, we must continue to invest time and effort to improve in our field. This deliberate focus ensures that we build on our strengths and achieve our long-term goals.

Simultaneously, we should also engage in new and unplanned activities in our daily or weekly routines. This keeps us open to new opportunities and experiences, fostering personal growth and adaptability. Embracing a variety of experiences allows us to discover new interests and potential avenues for success.

The best way to start this journey is to stop saying 'No'. However, not saying 'No' doesn't mean abandoning our deliberate strategy. Instead, it means integrating new experiences into our established goals and plans. By balancing our deliberate strategy with a willingness to explore and experiment, we can achieve a more dynamic and fulfilling life.

In essence, being open to new experiences while maintaining a clear direction helps us adapt to changing circumstances and seize opportunities as they arise. This balanced approach ensures that we continue to grow and succeed, both personally and professionally.

> *"We choose our joys and sorrows*
> *long before we experience them."*
>
> —**Khalil Gibran**

This is like when you are working and doing well in your organisation, and your friend calls and suggests starting a new venture. You might not be able to quit your job the next day, and that's understandable. However, you shouldn't completely say 'No' either.

Instead, you can time-box your commitment. Offer to help your friend for an hour a week, which is a manageable time commitment. Gradually, as the new business progresses, you can increase your involvement. This way, you can make a more informed decision about your level of commitment. By not saying 'No' upfront, you won't deny yourself the satisfaction of helping a friend and won't come across as unapproachable. Additionally, you gain valuable experiences from which you can learn a lot.

Avoiding an outright 'No' helps foster happiness and fulfilment. To summarise, start saying 'Yes' more often to situations, even when already committed to other responsibilities. This habit will reduce stress and lead to a more fulfilling life.

NOT LETTING EXTERNAL CIRCUMSTANCES AFFECT US

Finding balance in life often hinges on our ability to remain unaffected by external circumstances. This is easier said than done, and some might argue that such a person could be exploited by others. Additionally, one might question if it's even possible for a person to avoid feeling stifled, hurt or affected by what happens around them.

"Can we really remain unruffled in the face of external turmoil?"

Consider the loss of a loved one due to a fatal accident or illness, or experiencing a personal tragedy or health crisis. These events bring profound pain. Is it realistic to claim that someone could remain unaffected by such traumatic experiences? Is it possible to be human and not feel the sting of pain?

This topic is discussed in Chapter 6 instead of Chapter 1 because achieving such equanimity is not an easy task. It's a skill that requires time and practice to develop. One should start by handling smaller challenges that disturb one's peace of mind and gradually work up to more significant life challenges and traumatic events.

By building this resilience, step-by-step, we can strive to maintain our inner balance even amidst the storms of life.

Just like any skill that can be learned, I believe that people can become more resilient and find inner peace without letting external circumstances derail their happiness. The simplest way to understand this is to observe that no 2 people are affected equally or in the same way under similar circumstances.

We all know someone who, when faced with a challenging situation, maintains their calm, poise, and composure, unlike someone else who is very sensitive and easily affected by a tragic or traumatic situation. If we scrutinise why one person remains equanimous while another is easily disturbed, it becomes clear that the calm individual practices a certain mindset and skill. Their attitude and mindset towards the circumstances help them navigate the situation placidly.

Another example to instil confidence in the reader that achieving this is possible is the difference between a child's and an adult's reactions. If an adult snatches a toy from a toddler, the child will be very upset and wail loudly. However, an adult will not be as deeply affected if someone takes a toy from them. This indicates a difference in maturity levels.

As we grow and become adults, we become accustomed to our status, power in our organisation, titles, material possessions like houses, and relationships with our family, spouses, and children. This attachment affects our peace of mind when reality doesn't meet our expectations.

To develop the skill of not being affected by external circumstances, I would argue that one needs to start with simple things.

If we reflect on a day from the past week, we will likely identify many events that upset us. By looking back, we might agree that certain situations should ideally not have affected us as much. If we are honest with ourselves, we will realise that many people around us would not have been as affected by similar circumstances.

This reflection serves as a good starting point to identify the situations that affected us and consider how we can manage them better in the future. This skill is essential because if simple things deeply affect us and we are very sensitive to minor situations, it can have a significant impact on our well-being. For instance, someone gently scratching our car or involving us in a trivial discussion that makes us late for work, are minor incidents.

Research has shown that if we get emotionally disturbed by such simple events, our cognitive ability can drop precipitously. This can result in inefficient decision-making, such as crumbling under pressure, being unable to perform our best, or making mistakes like getting into an accident because our mind is preoccupied. This creates a vicious cycle where small things affect us emotionally, our mind becomes disturbed, and we are unable to think clearly, further deteriorating our situation and leading to greater unhappiness.

Therefore, the starting point is assessing how calm and happy we are initially. By identifying the small disturbances affecting our happiness and equanimity, we can take steps to control them. Failure to do so can lead to a loss of cognitive ability, resulting in poor decisions and worsening situations, perpetuating a vicious cycle of unhappiness.

Having established that it is possible and crucial to not let external circumstances affect our happiness, we can work towards gaining an internal sense of control. Being persistent and confident in adopting this strategy will help us remain happy, regardless of external situations. Developing this resilience will enable us to maintain our composure and make better decisions, ultimately leading to a more fulfilling and balanced life.

"Happiness is an inside job. Don't assign anyone else that much power over your life."
—Mandy Hale

I believe there are many effective strategies one can adopt to embark on the journey toward sustained happiness. Before adopting these strategies, it is essential to conduct a self-assessment to determine our maturity level and understand how much of our happiness we believe is controlled by external circumstances. We should reflect on the situations that rile us up and honestly evaluate whether those situations were trivial. It is also helpful to consider if there are people in our lives who can handle similar situations better than we did.

The first strategy to consider is simply avoiding situations that disturb our equanimity. This approach is especially beneficial for those who find it difficult to maintain self-control. By focusing on activities and environments that bring us happiness and do not affect us emotionally, we can gain better control over our emotional state. This immediately puts us on a positive trajectory, counteracting the negative spiral described earlier.

Another strategy is to practice mindfulness and meditation. These practices help us become more aware of our thoughts and emotions, allowing us to respond, rather than react, to challenging situations. Through regular meditation, we can train our minds to remain calm and centred, even when faced with stress.

Cultivating gratitude is also a powerful tool. By regularly reflecting on the positive aspects of our lives and expressing gratitude for them, we shift our focus away from what we lack or what disturbs us. This practice helps us build a more positive outlook, making us less susceptible to being upset by external circumstances.

Building strong relationships and seeking support from others can also enhance our resilience. Having a network of supportive friends and family members provides a buffer against stress and helps us navigate difficult times more effectively. Sharing our experiences and seeking advice from others who handle situations well can offer valuable insights and encouragement.

Setting realistic expectations and being flexible in our approach to life is another crucial strategy. Accepting that things may not always go as planned and being adaptable can reduce the frustration and disappointment we experience. This mindset helps us maintain a sense of control and balance, even when faced with unexpected challenges.

Lastly, engaging in activities that promote physical and mental well-being, such as regular exercise, healthy eating, and pursuing hobbies, can significantly enhance our overall happiness. These activities not only improve our physical health but also boost our mood and provide a sense of accomplishment and fulfilment.

So, for example, if there are individuals who consistently demotivate and make negative or sarcastic comments, and you find it difficult not to be affected by their remarks, it might be a good strategy to avoid such people. The reason for this is that, for whatever reasons, we may not yet have the maturity to remain unaffected by their negativity. This allows us to associate with those who motivate and inspire us. With our emotions in check, we can make better decisions, leading to a more positive and cheerful outlook on life.

> **"It is health that is real wealth,**
> **and not pieces of gold and silver."**
> **—Mahatma Gandhi**

Another strategy, in addition to avoiding negative situations and people, is to maintain a journal of reflections. I find this to be a very useful practice.

This involves simply reflecting on how our day went and replaying in our minds how we behaved in various situations. By doing this, we can think about how we might behave differently if similar situations arise in the future. This tool is valuable because it helps us assimilate real-life situations and mentally rehearse better responses.

If journaling isn't enough, finding a confidant can also be helpful. This could be someone like your mother, spouse, or another trusted person with whom you feel comfortable sharing personal situations. You can seek their opinion on how you could have handled the situation differently.

However, it's crucial to avoid seeking advice from someone who might give biased opinions or criticise rather than offer constructive feedback. For example, if you had an argument with someone and are feeling very angry, it's not helpful to seek advice from someone who tends to be critical. Instead, choose someone who will listen patiently and provide thoughtful, supportive suggestions on finding a solution.

So, we found that this process of assimilation and self-assessment helps us to be more prepared when similar situations arise in the future.

Reflect on how we behaved in various situations and consider how we would respond differently if the same situation occurs again. This reflection process should be done frequently and thoroughly. Each time, ask yourself additional questions about how you could improve your behaviour and responses in future similar situations.

By regularly engaging in these strategies, you can develop a stronger emotional resilience and a more positive outlook on life. This proactive approach ensures that you stay in control of your happiness and make better decisions, leading to a more fulfilling and cheerful life.

Asking ourselves, "What am I grateful for?" can help us navigate challenging situations effectively.

I found this to be a very useful tool. For example, imagine your boss gets upset with you at the office for making a mistake. You might either sulk through the rest of the meeting or respond to him inappropriately or aggressively. Later, as you reflect on the day, you consider how you could handle a similar situation differently in the future. A helpful way to guide your thoughts is to ask, "What am I grateful for?"

You might acknowledge that your boss behaved rudely and could have handled the situation better. However, you could also remind yourself of his mentorship and guidance, recalling instances when he supported you in similar situations. By writing these thoughts in your diary, it becomes easier to envision how you would behave differently and more constructively in future, similar situations.

Another useful tool for fostering positivity in your life is to reflect on past instances where your boss was kind to you. Also, think about generally positive situations. Recollecting all the good memories with your boss can be helpful. You might say,"Yes, I had this difficult situation with my boss, but I have many blessings in my life, such as good friends and other positive experiences."

Recognise that many good things have happened in your life. You are not living hand to mouth, you have good physical abilities and health, and you are blessed. Expressing gratitude for these things can shift your perspective.

When you reflect on all the positive aspects and express gratitude, it becomes easier to put challenging situations into perspective. This mindset helps you develop strategies to handle similar situations more effectively in the future.

And the reason we do this assimilation exercise is to train our minds. If you consider why we behave in certain ways and respond to situations as we do, it often stems from years of conditioning. These habits may have been picked up from our parents, bosses, or workplace environment. However, it's important to realise that it is not mandatory to behave in a way that negatively impacts our emotional well-being and health in the long run.

Therefore, we must start questioning this conditioning. The only way to challenge this conditioning and put ourselves on the right path is either to avoid particular situations or to actively engage our minds in thinking about and assimilating positive experiences.

By consciously reflecting on what we are grateful for and recognising the positive aspects of our lives, we can retrain our minds. This process helps us develop healthier responses to challenging situations, ultimately enhancing our emotional well-being and overall health.

> **"Happiness is not the absence of problems;**
> **it's the ability to deal with them."**
>
> **—Steve Maraboli**

This is very important so that when faced with difficult situations, we can consistently bring about more positive perspectives regarding the situation or the other person and gain control over ourselves. This approach will also prevent our emotional mindset from derailing our cognitive ability to make good decisions, placing us in a positive mode to live our lives happily.

As we discuss this, one of the questions that might come to the reader's mind is, "If we build this resilience and don't get affected by external situations, does that mean we need to start suppressing our emotions?"

For example, imagine someone acts very rudely towards us. Since we are practising the skill of not being disturbed by this kind of behaviour, wouldn't it be paramount to run away from the situation and avoid confrontation?

However, I would argue that controlling our emotions and not letting external circumstances affect us does not mean we should run away from the situation. These are 2 separate things. We should not let the situation control us; rather, we should control the situation.

In essence, it is about managing our emotional responses without suppressing them. It's about staying calm and composed, addressing the issue constructively and maintaining control over our reactions. This approach allows us to handle challenging situations effectively, while preserving our emotional well-being and cognitive clarity.

The key is to not let it affect us emotionally. This doesn't mean we're avoiding the situation. Instead, by maintaining our balance and poise, we confront the individual and communicate how their behaviour impacted us.

Perhaps we should start by reminding ourselves that this person has been good to us in many past instances, so we don't judge them solely based on this one incident. Once we regain our composure, we address the issue directly.

We might say, "Hey, Mr. [Name], I understand you were upset, but I felt hurt by the way you expressed yourself. Do you think your behaviour was harsh? I respect you a lot and want our relationship to strengthen. I believe your actions in the meeting could have been handled differently. Am I wrong in seeing it this way? What's your perspective?"

Or one could say, "I appreciate our working relationship and your support, but I felt hurt by your comments earlier. I believe it's important for us to communicate respectfully, even when we're frustrated. How can we ensure this doesn't happen again?"

By handling the situation calmly and constructively, we express our feelings without letting emotions take over. This method maintains respect and understanding in our relationships, ensuring that we stay in control of our emotional well-being.

> *"To be without some of the things you want is an indispensable part of Happiness."*
> —**Bertrand Russell**

By constructively confronting the person, we ensure that our relationship becomes stronger. We address the issue in a way that fosters understanding and growth, without letting it affect us negatively, either in the moment or afterward.

Additionally, we can coach the other person on their mistake in a way that maintains our emotional balance. This approach helps the other person see their mistake without feeling attacked, promoting a healthier dynamic. This is what I mean when I say we shouldn't let external circumstances affect us and steal our happiness. By maintaining our composure and addressing issues constructively, we protect our emotional well-being and build stronger, more respectful relationships.

THE PRESENT MOMENT IS NOT QUITE RIGHT

The present moment often goes unnoticed. Many individuals are either fixated on the future or preoccupied with the past. It is a common human tendency to not fully embrace the present. This habit can derail one's happiness and limit our ability to achieve balance and inner peace.

Let's delve deeper into this. Why are we always thinking about the future? While having goals is crucial, obsessively focusing on them can erode our sense of happiness and peace of mind. On the other hand, constantly living in the past is equally detrimental. When we dwell on past mistakes—whether our own or those of others—we become consumed by the situations we faced, impacting our present well-being.

It's important to understand that incessantly thinking about the past leads nowhere. Such thoughts will not change the current situation or shape the future.

While it is very tempting to think that we have complete control over the future, the number of variables that will affect it is significantly high, and most of them are beyond our control. Therefore, it is futile to plan excessively for the future and worry about it constantly. To find balance and inner peace, it is important not to dwell too much in the past or constantly fret about the future.

Instead, we should focus all our attention on the present moment. By concentrating on the present and dedicating our energy and focus to the tasks at hand, we can perform exceptionally well. When we consistently excel in our current activities, it naturally improves the quality of our future.

In essence, embracing the present and giving our best effort to each moment can lead to a more fulfilling and peaceful life. This approach not only enhances our current experiences but also sets a solid foundation for a better future. By living mindfully, we can break free from the cycles of past regrets and future anxieties, allowing us to truly enjoy and make the most of our lives.

A good way to assess whether we are sleepwalking through life, constantly thinking about the future or the past, is to ask ourselves: "Are we aware of each moment we are currently living?" or "Is our mind constantly disturbed by thoughts that have no relevance to our current situation?"

> **"A great obstacle to happiness is**
> **to expect too much happiness."**
> **—Bernard de Fontenelle**

Consider the example of driving. Often, while driving, on familiar routes, our minds drift to other thoughts. We may not even notice the journey until we reach our destination, as our minds were elsewhere, despite our eyes being on the road. This common experience highlights how frequently we are not truly present in our own lives.

One effective way to break this habit is through the practice of mindfulness. Often, we live each day reacting to situations as they arise. When there is a stimulus, we are conditioned to react immediately, without reflection. To break this chain, it can be beneficial to pause and not react instantly. Taking a moment to reflect on the stimulus or the situation allows us to respond more thoughtfully and intentionally.

Mindfulness helps us reclaim our focus on the present. It encourages us to be fully aware of our thoughts, emotions, and actions in each moment. By doing so, we can enjoy the richness of our current experiences and make more deliberate choices. This practice not only enhances our immediate well-being but also cultivates a deeper sense of peace and fulfilment in our lives.

It may not be feasible to pause and reflect in every situation, such as when driving and needing to quickly react to a pedestrian crossing the road. However, in less urgent circumstances, we can benefit greatly from taking a moment to pause and reflect on the situation. If it's not possible to do this in the moment, we should set aside time each day to reflect on the various events that have occurred.

During this reflection, we should ask ourselves: "Did we respond, or did we react?" Reacting is often an impulsive and less thoughtful way of dealing with situations, whereas responding is more deliberate and proactive.

When considering our responses, we should ask ourselves: "Did we practice empathy? If given a second chance, would we have responded more maturely?" By mentally role-playing the situation, we can explore different ways to handle similar scenarios in the future.

As we engage in this practice, we will begin to gain more control over our lives and start living in a more intentional and thoughtful manner. Reflecting on our actions and responses helps us to learn and grow, fostering a greater sense of self-awareness and emotional intelligence. This process enables us to navigate life's challenges with more grace and wisdom, ultimately leading to a more balanced and fulfilling life.

The Bhagavad Gita discusses 2 types of personalities inherent in every individual. Lord Krishna talks about the Asuri, or devilish tendencies, and the Deviga Sampadi, or godly tendencies. It is true that within each of us, despite our spiritual inclinations, no one is entirely good or bad.

> *"The secret of happiness is freedom;*
> *the secret of freedom is courage."*
> —**Carrie Jones**

When we react impulsively to a situation, we succumb to the Asuri Sampadi, or devilish tendencies. However, when we respond with calmness and empathy, we exercise our free will and emphasise our positive qualities. Reacting is characteristic of a tit-for-tat mentality.

For instance, if someone overtakes us while driving, our immediate reaction might be to speed up or shout at the other person. This is a reaction to the situation. A more proactive approach would be to pause and ask ourselves, "What are the possible reasons for the other person's behaviour?" Perhaps they are in a genuine hurry due to a medical emergency, or maybe they lack the maturity we possess. By excusing them in our minds, we avoid unnecessary conflict and maintain our peace.

Continuously reacting to situations keeps us in a cycle of negativity, making us no different from those who lack self-control. By choosing to respond thoughtfully, we exercise our Deviga Sampadi, or godly tendencies. This mindful approach helps us cultivate inner peace and happiness, leading to a more fulfilling life.

Ultimately, the goal is to find balance within ourselves, acknowledging both our positive and negative tendencies. By consciously choosing to respond, rather than react, we can lead a life guided by empathy, understanding, and wisdom. This practice not only enhances our well-being, but also positively influences those around us, creating a ripple effect of compassion and harmony in our interactions.

We must evolve our maturity. We can no longer behave like children when reacting to situations. By taking a pause and reflecting, whether during the situation or later, we continuously enhance our ability to respond, rather than react. This process requires us to be fully present in the moment.

If we are always preoccupied with the past or future, we will lack the emotional strength, self-awareness and self-control needed to handle situations effectively. Therefore, it is crucial to respond maturely to the challenges we face.

A helpful practice is to recognise and reflect on the instances each day where we reacted, instead of responding.

By investigating these moments, we can learn from them and prepare ourselves for similar situations in the future.

Ask yourself: How could I have responded differently? What emotions or thoughts influenced my reaction? How can I apply empathy and understanding in similar, future scenarios?

By consistently practising this reflection, we can develop greater emotional resilience and maturity. This self-awareness allows us to navigate life's challenges with a calm and thoughtful approach, ultimately leading to a more balanced and fulfilling life.

In summary, the journey towards maturity and inner peace involves:

- **Mindfulness:** Staying present and fully engaged in the current moment.
- **Reflection:** Regularly assessing our reactions and learning from them.
- **Empathy:** Understanding and considering the perspectives and needs of others.
- **Self-awareness:** Recognising our emotions and thoughts, and how they influence our behaviour.
- **Growth:** Continuously striving to respond, rather than react, fostering a more proactive and mature approach to life.

Through these practices, we can cultivate a life of greater emotional balance, inner peace, and meaningful connections with others. This journey is not about achieving perfection, but about making consistent efforts to grow and improve each day.

> *"Nobody cares if you're miserable,*
> *so you might as well be happy."*
> —Cynthia Nelms

FOCUS ON CREATION
VERSUS INFORMATION OVERLOAD

Many people struggle to find balance and inner peace because they are perpetually busy, neglecting to focus on their true passions. It's essential to recognise that no one needs to be fully informed about everything in the world. It's simply not feasible, nor is it beneficial to attempt such a feat. Yet, in the age of modern technology, we are constantly bombarded with information, which often leads to an overwhelming sense of information overload.

We join every conceivable WhatsApp group, eager to stay connected. The moment our phone rings, we feel an urgent need to answer every call. We read every news article, desperate to stay updated. This relentless stream of information clutters our minds, leaving us mentally exhausted and deprived of the clarity needed for meaningful endeavours.

Picture living in a house crammed with unnecessary items—90% of which are superfluous. Such a home would be chaotic and overwhelming. Similarly, when we expose ourselves to excessive information, our minds become cluttered and we lose the ability to focus on what truly matters.

To reclaim our peace of mind and find balance, it's crucial to simplify our lives. Identify one passion or goal you want to achieve and commit to it wholeheartedly. By saying no to the myriad distractions and unnecessary information, you create space for what truly matters. This focused approach allows you to invest your time and energy into areas that genuinely define your purpose and bring fulfilment.

Simplifying your life isn't just about reducing distractions; it's about making a conscious choice to prioritise what adds value and meaning. When you concentrate on your true passions and eliminate the noise, you pave the way for personal growth, creativity, and a deeper sense of inner peace. This mindful approach helps you to contribute meaningfully to the areas that matter most, ultimately leading to a more balanced and fulfilling life.

Consider the grandmasters like Magnus Carlsen or Viswanathan Anand. They are not expected to excel in every discipline; their brilliance lies in their mastery of chess. They have dedicated their lives to becoming world-class in this single area. It's not just acceptable, but admirable, that they focus on excelling in one discipline rather than spreading themselves thin across many. Their choice to concentrate on chess has allowed them to reach the pinnacle of their field.

Similarly, in our lives, we should strive to identify a central goal and dedicate ourselves to it. Chasing too many ambitions can lead to a fragmented and less fulfilling life. While it's beneficial to have hobbies for relaxation, our primary focus should be on one or 2 areas where we aim to achieve world-class excellence.

The journey to mastery is not a quick one. As the saying goes, it takes approximately 10,000 hours to become proficient in any field. This translates to about 10 years of dedicated effort. To reach a world-class level, we must commit ourselves deeply to pursuits that give our lives meaning and purpose.

This focused dedication is what separates those who excel from those who remain average. By pouring our time and energy into our chosen field, we not only improve our skills but also find deeper satisfaction and fulfilment. The process of becoming world-class is about more than just putting in the hours; it's about passion, perseverance, and a relentless pursuit of excellence.

In today's world, where distractions are plentiful and information is abundant, it becomes even more crucial to protect our time and focus. Simplifying our lives by concentrating on fewer, more meaningful pursuits allows us to channel our efforts effectively. This not only enhances our potential for success, but also brings a profound sense of inner peace and balance.

> ***"We can't control the world. We can only (barely) control our reactions to it. Happiness is largely a choice, not a right or entitlement."***
>
> **—David C. Hill**

Hence, we must reduce the clutter. Once we do, our minds will be much more at ease. We should not fall victim to social pressures. There will always be someone advising us on what we should do, trying to characterise and amplify our weaknesses.

Who doesn't have a weakness? It is okay to have a weakness. Not everyone needs to be the same. Just as not all fingers on our hand are equally sized, there is nothing wrong with being unique. Each individual is gifted in something, and that is what is important.

It is our moral duty and obligation to develop our strengths. Our unique set of characteristics aligns with our goals. We should not waste time on things that we can neither excel at nor that align with our goals.

MATERIAL THINGS DON'T GIVE LASTING PEACE

I remember when my friend Ashwin bought his dream car. He was thrilled, driving around as if he'd just won the lottery. But 3 days later, I asked how he liked it. He sighed and said, "The cup holders could be better."

It's a curious thing about happiness—no matter if we're dreaming of a new car, a bigger house, or even a coveted promotion, the joy we feel from these achievements is often short-lived. We find ourselves in a perpetual chase, running after one material goal after another. And it's not just the tangible things; even when we land that big promotion, the excitement fades after a few days, and soon, we're on to the next pursuit.

Studies show that these material gains don't bring us lasting happiness. The secret to true balance and inner peace lies in discovering a deeper meaning in life. It's not about the external motivators; we need to embark on a journey within ourselves to find true happiness.

Imagine a beautiful irony: in prisons, solitary confinement is deemed the harshest punishment. Even the most hardened criminals dread solitude and prefer the company of fellow inmates. Humans are social creatures, and the fear of loneliness underscores our need for connection. But, here's the twist— real happiness isn't found in our relationships with others, not even with our spouses or children, nor in accumulating material wealth.

So, how does this paradox work? If material things don't bring lasting joy, why do we all participate in this relentless rat race? The truth is, we've been looking in the wrong places. We believe that external achievements will fill the void, but genuine fulfilment comes from within. By shifting our focus inward, we can break free from the cycle of perpetual chasing and discover a more profound and enduring happiness.

Why then, do we continue to compete, striving for the next shiny object or accolade? It's time to pause and reflect. The answers we seek are not out there in the world, but within ourselves. In finding inner peace, we unlock the true essence of happiness, unshackled from the endless pursuit of the material.

Research clearly shows that up to a certain point— specifically around 75,000 pounds a year in the UK or roughly one and a half lakh rupees per month in India, adjusted for purchasing power parity—an increase in wealth can indeed bring incremental happiness. However, once your income exceeds this threshold, additional wealth does not equate to more happiness.

So why do we still chase after more? If material possessions aren't the key to lasting joy, what's driving this endless pursuit?

The answer lies in the journey rather than the destination. When we set our sights on a goal, the happiness we experience is not from achieving it, but from the process of working towards it.

Chapter 1 highlighted the importance of having a meaningful goal in life. Having a clear objective gives our minds something to focus on, steering us away from the clutter of countless thoughts. It's said that the human mind generates over 60,000 thoughts each day, many of which we're not even consciously aware of. By concentrating on the task at hand or living fully in the present moment, we can declutter our minds.

This mental focus allows us to improve our skills and, over time, achieve world-class performance. Such excellence often leads to external success, which is recognised by others. However, true happiness comes not from the accolades, but from the joy of performing the task itself and the journey it entails.

Consider this: the satisfaction derived from the journey is profound. As we consistently work on our tasks, honing our skills and improving our competence, we start to enjoy the process. This enjoyment is a key aspect of true happiness. The journey, with all its challenges and learning experiences, brings a sense of fulfilment that the end goal alone cannot provide.

In essence, external success might be visible to others, but our true happiness lies in the performance and the process of the task. It's not the goal that ultimately brings contentment, but the journey towards achieving it. So, rather than fixating on the destination, we should embrace and find joy in the path we take to get there.

Let's revisit the example of aiming for a quicker promotion. It's perfectly fine to work hard towards achieving that promotion, but it's crucial to understand that the promotion itself won't bring lasting happiness. The true joy lies in the effort and dedication we put into working towards that goal.

This brings us back to the importance of having a meaningful goal, as discussed in Chapter 1. A goal gives our minds a clear direction and prevents us from getting distracted by the myriad of thoughts that clutter our minds daily. By focusing on a lofty purpose, we channel our energies towards something meaningful, which inherently brings us satisfaction and fulfilment.

Think of it as climbing a mountain. While reaching the summit is exhilarating, the true essence of the experience is in the climb itself—the challenges we overcome, the skills we hone, and the breathtaking moments we encounter along the way. Similarly, in our professional and personal lives, setting and pursuing meaningful goals enriches our journey and makes it worthwhile.

So, aim high and set ambitious goals, but savour the journey. Embrace the process, the small victories, and the learning experiences. This mindset shift—from being destination-focused to journey-focused—can transform the way we perceive and pursue happiness. It helps us find joy in the present moment, appreciate our progress and, ultimately, lead a more fulfilling life.

> *"The world is full of people looking for spectacular happiness while they snub contentment."*
>
> —**Doug Larson**

CONCLUSION

In Chapter 6, we embarked on a journey to understand the significance of balance and inner peace in our pursuit of happiness and fulfilment. We explored the concept of unhappiness as a by-product of attachments and the profound impact of learning to let go. By reflecting on our mortality and practising detachment, we can cultivate a sense of equanimity and joy. Additionally, we emphasised the power of saying 'yes' to life's opportunities and remaining open to new experiences, which fosters personal growth and resilience. Finally, we examined the importance of not letting external circumstances dictate our happiness, focusing instead on our internal responses and emotional resilience. By integrating mindfulness, gratitude, and a proactive approach to life's challenges, we can maintain a state of balance and inner peace, leading to a more meaningful and joyful existence.

KEY TAKEAWAYS

1. **Unhappiness and Attachment:** Recognise that unhappiness often stems from our attachments. Letting go of these attachments can lead to greater inner peace and joy.

2. **Mindfulness and Self-awareness:** Practice mindfulness to stay present in the moment. Reflect on your thoughts and emotions without judgement, allowing for a more balanced and composed response to life's challenges.

3. **Saying 'Yes' to Life:** Embrace new experiences and opportunities. Saying 'yes' can lead to personal growth, resilience, and a deeper sense of fulfilment.

4. **Detachment and Inner Peace:** Understand the transient nature of material possessions and relationships. Focus on cultivating inner peace and balance by letting go of attachments.

5. **Responding vs. Reacting:** Develop the skill of responding thoughtfully to situations rather than reacting impulsively. This proactive approach fosters emotional resilience and better decision-making.

6. **Focus on Creation:** Avoid information overload by simplifying your life and focusing on your true passions. Dedicate your time and energy to pursuits that bring meaning and fulfilment.

7. **Embrace the Journey:**   Recognise that true happiness lies in the journey, not just the destination. Set meaningful goals and enjoy the process of working towards them.

8. **Gratitude and Positivity:** Cultivate gratitude by reflecting on the positive aspects of your life. This practice helps shift your focus from what you lack to what you have, fostering a more positive outlook.

By integrating these key takeaways into your daily life, you can achieve a state of balance and inner peace, ultimately leading to a happier and more fulfilling existence.

CHAPTER 7

QUALITIES THAT DEFINE A HAPPY LIFE

INTRODUCTION:

In the preceding 6 chapters, we explored the framework for achieving happiness and the essential steps in this pursuit. We began by delving into the concept of flow and how it helps us discover our sense of purpose and duty in life, asking ourselves, "What are we good at, and what have we accomplished?"

Next, we examined the idea that the ends do not justify the means, emphasising the importance of developing the right attitude and mindset to achieve our purpose and higher goals. We also identified certain practices to avoid as they can derail our sense of happiness and well-being.

In chapter 4, we discussed the importance of taking others along on our journey. We cannot be solitary horses trying to find our way; instead, we must build relationships and find supporters to sustain our happiness and pursuit of goals. Chapter 5 highlighted the need to develop a sense of detachment and resilience in life, essential for navigating challenges without losing our equilibrium.

In chapter 6, we explored how to find a sense of inner peace and a feeling of abundance, recognising that true contentment comes from within.

Finally, in this chapter, we will look at the qualities that can act as a checklist for finding inner peace and happiness. These qualities, when nurtured, can guide us towards a fulfilling and joyful life.

> *"The essence of philosophy is that a man should live*
> *so that his happiness shall depend as little as*
> *possible on external things."*
>
> —Epictetus

So, let us get started.

DEFINE WHAT HAPPINESS MEANS TO YOU

The first and most important quality of a happy life is understanding what happiness means to us. This is a deeply personal question: what happiness means to me might not mean happiness to someone else. Therefore, we must become comfortable answering this question for ourselves and be completely at peace with the answer we find.

For example, does happiness mean money and fame to you? If so, then you should pursue it unapologetically and with utmost passion. If happiness means creating an impact in the social sector, don't let others define what happiness should mean to you. It is a great misfortune to pursue a mission in life that doesn't align with our core purpose and our own definition of happiness.

Many people today pursue careers like engineering or medicine without realising that these professions might not truly drive them. They don't want to be engineers or doctors, but societal or parental pressure pushes them into these fields. This scenario is especially common in India, where parents often push their children into engineering and medical science, believing it will make them successful and happy.

As a result, some individuals end up becoming engineers despite lacking any real aptitude or passion for the field. This issue was poignantly and humorously highlighted in the movie "3 Idiots."

Thus, it is crucial to get comfortable with our own definition of happiness. Equally important is understanding that happiness itself is a journey, a progression from a lower state of maturity to a higher sense of maturity. Embracing this journey allows us to pursue our true passions and live a fulfilling life.

So, let us look at it in more detail.

> ***"My family didn't have a lot of money, and
> I'm grateful for that. Money is the longest
> route to happiness."***
>
> —**Evangeline Lilly**

DIFFERENT TYPES OF HAPPINESS

In this paragraph, I would like to elaborate on different types of happiness. By no means is this a complete list, but it will provide insight into the various kinds of happiness that exist.

The first and most basic form of happiness is derived from material comfort, which gives us sensory pleasure. Let's call this "Sensory Happiness". For example, receiving a cherished gift like a toy or a car on our birthday makes us very happy. The excitement of knowing that someone has thought about our happiness brings us a lot of joy.

The second form of happiness, which is a bit more advanced and harder to attain, comes from success or holding a position of power in life. For instance, getting promoted to a new role or obtaining a job with additional responsibilities and a team to lead is something most people would welcome. This kind of achievement provides us with a sense of happiness and accomplishment.

The third type of happiness arises when we become an expert or are recognised as one. For example, highly qualified surgeons are often regarded as lifesavers by many people who seek their expertise. Similarly, top management consultants are sought after by leading companies worldwide for their ability to diagnose business issues and recommend strategic paths. Achieving expertise in our chosen field, whether in sports or any other area, can also lead to a profound sense of accomplishment and happiness.

The next type of happiness is born out of love, relationships, and connections we share with others. This is a profound sense of happiness evident in the birth of a child. The closeness and connection we feel with our loved ones and family members stem from unconditional love. Regardless of how our parents or children look or their capabilities, we love them truly and unconditionally. Their actions, no matter how small, bring us immense joy. This happiness also extends to the success of others or when someone sincerely wishes us on our birthday. It's not just the material gifts, but the heartfelt wishes from those who truly care about us that bring great happiness.

The last type of happiness I would like to highlight is the state of complete inner peace, a state of abundance reached through a high level of maturity. This is the kind of happiness often exhibited by spiritual gurus. I am particularly inspired by Sri Sri Ravi Shankar. Whenever I see him on TV, he exudes confidence and inner peace. His face radiates tranquillity and happiness.

While exploring these different types of happiness, it is crucial to understand that what makes us truly happy is our sense of maturity. Maturity is not merely a function of age; I have encountered very old people who still exhibit immaturity. True maturity involves a deep understanding and acceptance of life, leading to a lasting and profound sense of happiness.

This is because they have not been exposed to knowledge or have not been mentored by individuals with a higher level of emotional maturity. For example, we can't expect a child to display a higher sense of maturity by becoming an expert or holding a position of power. A child finds happiness in receiving even a small gift. A simple material gift can bring them immense joy, making them dance with excitement. However, as we grow older, our fascination with toys diminishes. The toys that once enthralled us as children no longer hold our interest. Instead, we look for bigger toys, such as a larger car or a bigger house. These are adult toys suited to our grown-up desires.

But ultimately, we should realise that we reach a higher sense of maturity when we stop letting our happiness be determined by costlier toys. At this point, we experience a higher state of happiness through detachment.

An important aspect of this realisation is how we raise our children. We should not rob them of the joys of childhood by denying them sensory pleasures like toys or cars they long for. However, overindulgence in material pleasures, without teaching them the value of money, can lead to poor parenting. This results in children not understanding that some things need to be earned, and that there are higher values beyond material gifts.

Therefore, moderation is essential in raising our children. Just as we practice moderation with them, we should also be mindful of our own well-being and happiness by moderating our attachment to material pleasures. Obsessively focusing on the next promotion, the next biggest car, or the next bigger house robs us of higher levels of happiness associated with maturity. True happiness lies in inner bliss, the love and connections we seek, and the pursuit of knowledge and wisdom.

So, it is true that we must strive to seek a higher state of happiness, not only for ourselves but also for our loved ones. At the same time, it is essential to be congruent with our current state of maturity. For instance, if we have not yet achieved a higher state of maturity, we should not deprive ourselves or our children of sensory happiness in our quest to reach it.

It is equally important to avoid being judgemental about others' sources of happiness. How can we judge someone for finding happiness in reading a book, or for not becoming an expert in a particular field? Perhaps their maturity levels and definitions of happiness are different from ours.

> *"Happiness lies in the joy of achievement*
> *and the thrill of creative effort."*
> **—Franklin D. Roosevelt**

We must recognise that everyone's definition of happiness can vary. Accepting this diversity of perspectives allows us to appreciate the unique ways others find joy and fulfilment.

In this chapter, our discussion focuses on discovering our personal areas of happiness. What does happiness mean to us? Where do we stand on the maturity curve in terms of happiness?

"Are we still like a child, or are we on a quest to seek higher forms of happiness?"

"Are we congruent with our current maturity?"

If we are not congruent, we are out of sync, like a fish out of water. It is vital to understand and embrace our current state of happiness while continually striving for higher, more profound levels of joy and contentment. This journey of self-discovery and growth in understanding happiness is essential for leading a fulfilled and balanced life.

> *"There can be no happiness if the things we believe*
> *in are different from the things we do."*
> **—Freya Stark**

WRITING DOWN YOUR GOALS

To truly achieve happiness, it's essential to define our goals and milestones with clarity and precision. Imagine setting a vision for the next 3 years, breaking it down into what you aim to achieve in the next year, the next month, and even the next 7 days. While it might seem overwhelming to jot down all these goals daily, focusing on the most significant milestones each morning can be incredibly beneficial.

Starting the day by writing down your key goals provides a powerful motivation to leap out of bed with enthusiasm. I've found this practice transformative in my life. Every morning, with a cup of coffee in hand, I sit down and document my goals. This simple ritual does wonders.

There are several compelling reasons to make this a daily habit. Firstly, it sets a positive tone for the day. Our minds are often preoccupied with worries and negative thoughts, fixating on worst-case scenarios that are beyond our control. By focusing on our goals, we shift our mindset to a more positive outlook, concentrating on what we can control, rather than what we can't.

Why spend your day fretting over uncontrollable factors when you can start with a clear, positive intention? Writing down your goals each morning not only helps you stay focused, but also enhances your overall well-being by fostering a sense of purpose and control.

Secondly, by writing down our goals, we subconsciously align our day with our objectives. This natural prioritisation ensures that our actions support our goals without needing constant, explicit reminders. Of course, if we can explicitly prioritise our day, it's even better. By simply jotting down your goals each morning, you can more easily say no to tasks that don't contribute to your aspirations.

Another advantage is the clarity it provides. Defining your goals helps you understand what happiness means to you, what your purpose is, and why you're doing what you're doing. This is crucial because each day brings its share of challenges and rough patches. What keeps us motivated through tough times is the daily reminder of our higher purpose and goals.

> **"Happiness is a by-product of an effort to make someone else happy."**
> **—Gretta Brooker Palmer**

For example, if your goal is to achieve great health, you'll be more committed to doing those extra reps during your workout. You'll know that each extra effort brings you closer to your larger goal.

Writing down your goals is key to successful strategy execution. It helps us stay consistent with our strategic intent, both in our personal and professional lives. It ensures we focus our resources on what truly matters and remain aligned with our broader objectives. By starting each day with a clear set of goals, we set ourselves up for a day filled with purpose, positivity and progress.

DEVELOP STRONG HABITS AND STICK TO THEM

By nature, our minds lean towards laziness. This isn't just a casual observation but a well-documented fact, explored by many scholars. One of the most notable among them is Nobel laureate Daniel Kahneman. In his renowned book, *Thinking, Fast and Slow*, he introduces the concepts of System 1 and System 2, which help explain this tendency.

System 1 is our autopilot mode. It's the part of our brain that handles routine tasks effortlessly, like driving a car or swimming. These activities become second nature to us, requiring little conscious thought. On the other hand, System 2 is our logical and creative mind. It's the part we engage when we need to solve complex problems or think critically. However, our brains, being efficient energy conservers, prefer not to use System 2 too often.

This preference stems from our brain's physiological need to conserve energy. Constantly engaging System 2 would be mentally exhausting, leaving us overwhelmed and unable to function effectively. Historically, this energy conservation was vital for survival. Imagine our ancestors encountering a tiger. There was no time to ponder the best course of action; immediate reaction, driven by System 1, was essential for survival.

System 1, therefore, can be seen as our primitive brain, honed over millennia to react swiftly to danger. In modern times, though, while we may not face tigers, this system still governs much of our behaviour. The challenge lies in recognising when to switch gears and engage System 2, our more thoughtful and deliberate mind.

To cultivate strong habits, we must consciously activate System 2, especially when forming new routines. Initially, this requires effort and energy, but over time, these habits can transition into System 1 territory, becoming automatic and effortless. This blend of deliberate practice and eventual automation is key to personal growth and efficiency.

By understanding and leveraging the dynamics between System 1 and System 2, we can develop strong habits and stick to them, ultimately enhancing our productivity and well-being.

So, as we can see, System 1 excels at tasks once it has learned how to perform them. It operates with remarkable efficiency and precision. A famous example of this is a video featuring the legendary footballer Cristiano Ronaldo. In the video, the lights are turned off, and Ronaldo is tasked with scoring a goal in complete darkness. Remarkably, he succeeds multiple times, far outshining those who are less trained or skilled. Without even seeing the ball, Ronaldo can judge its trajectory and score, showcasing System 1's adaptability and proficiency in executing learned tasks flawlessly. This ability to perform under challenging conditions is what sets great performers apart.

To harness the power of System 1 in our daily lives, it is crucial to develop strong habits. When we cultivate habits through repetition, we become exceptionally skilled at them, potentially reaching world-class levels of proficiency. This automation of everyday tasks not only boosts our performance but also reduces stress. Constantly worrying about how to tackle routine tasks can drain our mental energy and diminish our happiness.

Consider the stress involved in tackling an entirely new and unfamiliar task. Without prior experience or skill, our performance is likely to be subpar, leading to frustration and anxiety. If every task we faced were of this nature, we would quickly become overwhelmed and stressed.

Developing strong habits mitigates this issue. By automating routine tasks, we free up cognitive resources for more complex and creative endeavours. This balance allows us to maintain our well-being while enhancing productivity. Embracing the power of habit not only makes us more efficient, but also enriches our lives by reducing unnecessary stress and allowing us to focus on what truly matters.

> **"Now and then, it's good to pause in
> our pursuit of happiness and just be happy."**
> **—Guillaume Apollinaire**

No wonder so many people feel extremely stressed or burnt out in their daily routines. They are constantly engaged in tasks at which they are not proficient, leading to feelings of being overwhelmed.

One of the best ways to alleviate this stress and create more time for the activities we love is to develop a set of good habits. These habits can simplify daily decision-making, reducing the mental burden and freeing up cognitive resources. For instance, if we prioritise our day by allocating time for family, health, and personal time, we create a balanced life. However, it's crucial to stick to the schedule set for these activities without constant changes.

In professional settings, particularly in leadership roles, it's beneficial to establish clear rules and boundaries that empower team members to make decisions independently. This approach minimises the need for leaders to be involved in every minor issue, allowing them to focus on more strategic tasks. Similarly, when investing in the stock market, having a well-defined set of rules can help in making more objective and less emotionally-driven decisions.

By creating structured routines and delegating effectively, we can reduce stress and enhance productivity. This method not only benefits individual well-being but also improves overall team performance. Establishing strong habits is about building a framework within which we operate efficiently, allowing us to focus on what truly matters and enjoy a more fulfilling life.

For example, consider the strategy of investing in the stock market. By tracking specific indicators and matrices for a company, you can make informed decisions without getting bogged down by the daily fluctuations of the market. Once these matrices align with your investment criteria, you can confidently invest, rather than constantly worrying about market volatility. This strategy is widely adopted by successful traders who stick to their systems, regardless of market conditions.

The principle of adhering to established rules also extends to ethical practices. Renowned author Clayton Christensen, in his insightful book *How Will You Measure Your Life?*, emphasises the importance of being 100% committed to your values rather than compromising even 1% of the time. He argues that it is easier to be right all the time than to be right most of the time. Compromising on values in seemingly minor situations can create stress and establish a habit of slipping up in more significant circumstances.

Consider the simple act of obeying traffic signals. If the light is red, you stop. This might seem straightforward, but it reflects a deeper commitment to rules. A personal experience I had illustrates this point. Late one Saturday night on a Mumbai road, I stopped my car at a red light. Suddenly, an auto-rickshaw crashed into the back of my car. The driver, visibly annoyed, asked me, "Why did you stop at the signal?" Bewildered, I responded, "The light was red, so I stopped." He retorted, "It's nighttime, and no one stops at signals at night."

Despite the heavy dent in my car that required repairs, I chose not to argue further. The auto driver firmly believed I was in the wrong for obeying the traffic signal. This incident highlights how adherence to rules, even when it seems inconvenient or unnecessary, is crucial. It prevents chaos and maintains order.

My belief is clear and unwavering: when there's a rule, we must follow it 100% of the time, not 99.99%. This steadfast commitment instils a profound sense of comfort and security. By prioritising our daily routines, like getting a good night's sleep, over the stress of hiding or bending the rules, we foster a healthier, more balanced life.

This principle of absolute adherence extends beyond just following rules; it applies to speaking up, especially during meetings or discussions. There are times when expressing our views might be unpopular or uncomfortable, particularly if it involves confronting someone who has done something wrong. Despite the potential for a negative reaction, it is crucial to gently, but firmly, express why their actions were incorrect. This kind of confrontation, though difficult, is necessary if we believe in the righteousness of our stance.

Developing a set of habits based on our core values and our understanding of right and wrong is vital for leading a happy and fulfilling life. These habits should be non-negotiable, adhered to without exceptions. This consistency is the third most important quality one must cultivate. By sticking to our principles 100% of the time, we create a foundation of integrity and reliability.

When we follow our values and habits unwaveringly, we significantly reduce the stress in our lives. This approach allows us to go to bed each night with a sense of satisfaction, knowing we did the right thing and gave our best effort that day, whether at work or in our personal lives. This commitment to our values not only brings peace of mind but also builds a life of genuine fulfilment and happiness.

In conclusion, developing strong habits and sticking to them, whether in investing, ethical practices, or everyday tasks, significantly reduces stress and enhances performance. By automating routine decisions through well-established habits, we free our minds for more important and creative endeavours. This approach not only makes us more efficient, but also fosters a life of integrity and fulfilment.

> *"Happiness is a matter of one's most ordinary*
> *and everyday mode of consciousness being busy*
> *and lively and unconcerned with self."*
> —**Iris Murdoch**

SPEAK UP WHEN IT ONLY TRULY MATTERS

Words are power. Used well, they can inspire a nation, change a life, and make the world a better place. But words also hold the potential to destroy a person, corrupt society, and disturb the tranquillity and well-being of others.

A crucial quality that every individual must continuously develop and hone is knowing when and how to speak up—and, perhaps most importantly, when to stay silent and let things go.

This skill is vital for leading a happy life and building strong relationships.

I've found that applying 4 filters before reacting to a situation and expressing ourselves can be incredibly beneficial. The first filter we should use when we start speaking is to ask ourselves, "Are we speaking the truth?"

We must always speak the truth, no matter the consequences. While this might sound cliché, I've seen many individuals speak the truth most of the time, but not all the time. This inconsistency must be avoided at all costs. If we can't speak the truth, we should choose silence over lies.

The question to ask ourselves is: "Are we truthful in every situation, in every circumstance, and at every point in time?" Speaking something untrue leaves our minds feeling guilty. Even if we get away with a lie, our minds will remain perturbed and fearful, worrying that the lie, however trivial, will be uncovered one day. It's simply not worth the time and energy.

We need to promise ourselves that whenever we speak, we should always speak the truth – 100% of the time, not stopping or being content at 99%.

The second filter before we start speaking is to question ourselves, "Are we gentle in our choice of words?"

Even when we speak the truth, our words need to be gentle. Our righteousness in correcting something or speaking the truth does not give us the right to be harsh. Feeling strongly about our correctness does not grant us the authority to speak harshly to others. We can and should speak the truth, but let's also make it a habit to convey it gently, so as not to hurt another individual's self-esteem.

A great example of speaking the truth while being firm yet gentle can be found in the autobiography of the Father of our nation, Mohandas Karamchand Gandhi. In his book *My Experiments with Truth*, Gandhi recounts numerous situations where, even under challenging circumstances, he always spoke his mind, always spoke the truth, and did so in a gentle, understanding and empathetic manner.

Throughout his book, Gandhi recalls various incidents where he had to have very tough conversations—with his wife, his family, his party members, or with the British. Yet, he always maintained an amicable tone. His ability to balance firmness with gentleness is a testament to the power of kind words and a gentle approach.

This is because the moment we are harsh, it will again play on our minds, leading to feelings of misery and regret about our behaviour. Therefore, it is crucial that while we speak the truth, we do so in a soft and gentle tone.

I have observed parents who are sometimes very harsh with their children. Children are incredibly impressionable, so when we teach them what is right or wrong, we must be gentle and soft in our tone. No one, not even parents, has the right to be rude or insensitive in their handling of kids. The way we communicate with children shapes their understanding of the world and their self-worth. Gentle guidance fosters a sense of security and self-confidence.

Another crucial aspect of speaking the truth is when we give feedback as leaders to our subordinates. Feedback should not be delivered in a manner that completely erodes the recipient's self-confidence. Conversely, withholding constructive criticism, or even worse, offering false praise when it is undeserved, leads to a loss of credibility over time. Leaders must find a balance between being honest and being encouraging.

Moreover, giving feedback to our superiors requires the same level of care. If we disagree with something, we must be bold enough to speak the truth and hold up a mirror to reflect the reality, but we must do so tactfully and gently. Constructive criticism should be framed in a way that is respectful and aims to contribute positively to the overall goals of the organisation.

The third filter we should apply before we start speaking is to consider: "Are we speaking to help, heal, or hurt? Even if we are speaking the truth gently, is our intention to do good, especially to the person we are addressing?"

Our words and actions should always aim for the welfare of society. Often, people hesitate to speak up because they are unsure of how the recipient will react, leading them to avoid difficult conversations. This third filter encourages us to be straightforward and ensures we remain focused on the bigger picture.

By examining our intentions and ensuring they are rooted in kindness and the desire to help, we can navigate challenging dialogues more effectively and constructively.

When we communicate, our intentions matter greatly. Are we aiming to help someone grow, heal from a difficult experience, or are we unintentionally or intentionally trying to hurt them? Our words should always aim to uplift and support, never to wound or break someone down. This filter helps us remain mindful of the impact our words can have on others.

Finally, the fourth filter is to ask ourselves, "Is it necessary to speak at all?"

The last filter is crucial: ensuring that whatever we say does not disturb the tranquillity and peace of mind of the person we are speaking to or the environment around us. This filter can be challenging to apply, especially since it often conflicts with the need to be truthful. It's important to recognise that not everyone shares the same values or level of maturity.

We must assess whether the person receiving our feedback is in the right frame of mind and capable of handling it. For instance, many elements of this book might not resonate with a very young audience because they may lack the maturity to fully grasp the concepts discussed.

Therefore, it is essential to continuously evaluate whether the recipient has the maturity and the intent to constructively use our perspective. Providing feedback to the wrong person can lead to it being misused or causing harm.

To maintain our own sense of well-being and tranquillity, we should avoid offering unsolicited advice or feedback that may not be beneficial. Assess the situation carefully to determine if sharing the truth will be constructive for the recipient. In doing so, we ensure that our words are both considerate and impactful, fostering a positive exchange.

Sometimes, the most powerful response is silence. Not every thought needs to be voiced, and not every situation requires our input. By choosing silence over unnecessary words, we can avoid conflicts and misunderstandings. Silence, when used wisely, can be a powerful tool for reflection and understanding.

Sometimes, it is futile and not in our best interest to engage with someone who is inherently untrustworthy. Such individuals often twist facts and create nuisances that can harm our cause. It's wiser to invest our time and energy elsewhere. This fourth filter helps us conserve our creative energy and protect our well-being. People with negative or egoistic mindsets tend to prioritise their own beliefs over listening to others, which only breeds negativity.

Instead of blaming the world or others for not understanding our point of view, we should ask ourselves if we properly assessed the situation and the person before sharing our thoughts. This self-reflection can prevent unnecessary conflicts and misunderstandings.

In every interaction, let us remember the power of our words and strive to use them wisely. Speak up when it truly matters and do so with honesty and kindness. This approach will lead to a life filled with meaningful connections and a legacy of positive influence.

To summarise, we should apply 4 filters to make our communications more effective:

1. **Always Speak the Truth:** Honesty forms the foundation of meaningful communication.
2. **Convey Things Gently:** Ensure that our words are kind and considerate.
3. **Have the Right Intention:** Share feedback with the intent to help and support, not to harm.
4. **Preserve Tranquillity:** Ensure our words do not disturb the peace and well-being of others.

By consistently applying these filters, we can communicate more effectively, fostering positive interactions and understanding.

> *"The foolish man seeks happiness in the distance,*
> *the wise grows it under his feet."*
>
> —James Oppenheim

SEEK CHALLENGES TO LEARN AND GROW

One of the most remarkable traits I've noticed in happy and successful people is their relentless pursuit of challenges as a means to learn and grow. They are always on a quest to acquire new knowledge, never shying away from the possibility of failure.

This admirable quality is especially evident in young children. Their eagerness to learn something new and their passion for pursuing diverse interests are truly inspiring. They constantly ask questions, seek to understand new things and strive to improve themselves.

However, as children grow up, they often become institutionalised, led to believe they cannot pursue multiple interests simultaneously. But this is not entirely true. The inner child within us still craves to explore new avenues and possesses an infinite potential to push the boundaries of conventional wisdom and overcome limiting beliefs.

By embracing challenges and maintaining a curious mindset, we can continue to learn and grow, just like the inquisitive children we once were. This continuous pursuit of knowledge and self-improvement is the key to a fulfilling and successful life.

We must continuously seek out new activities that rejuvenate us, perhaps developing interests that differ from our current focus. This exploration can lead to personal growth and new dimensions of creativity. For instance, it's believed that Einstein spent a significant amount of time playing the violin. His passion for music might have enhanced his creativity, contributing to his genius in unexpected ways.

Another inspiring example is N. Chandrasekaran, the chairman of Tata Group. He started running in his late forties, an age when many people think it's too late to pick up new activities. Yet, he became a marathon runner, finding clarity and numerous health benefits in the process. If someone as busy as the chairman of Tata Group could find time to develop a new hobby, what's stopping us from pursuing new interests?

Consider also Dr Bala Balachandran, the Dean of Great Lakes Institute of Management. He founded the institute around 2005, believing in the need for a quality management school in South India, which lacked IIMs at the time. Despite being in his late sixties and a distinguished professor at Kellogg School of Management, he pursued this vision. Today, the Great Lakes Institute of Management is consistently ranked among the top 10 management institutes in India.

These examples illustrate that there is no age limit to exploring something new. Regardless of our age or busy schedules, we must find time to follow our passions. By doing so, we can develop our hobbies into something significant and impactful, not just for ourselves, but for society at large.

Never give up on your passions and interests. By continuously experimenting and seeking new challenges, we can turn our hobbies into meaningful pursuits that enrich our lives and those around us.

LIST DOWN THE THINGS THAT MAKE YOU HAPPY AND JUST DO IT

In our quest for happiness, we often overlook the simplest ways to achieve it, making the pursuit seem more complicated than it truly is. One of the key observations about happy people is their clarity regarding activities that bring them joy. They identify these activities and incorporate them regularly into their daily routine. It's that simple!

Just like a machine requires recharging, care, and maintenance, our minds need to be rejuvenated to keep our energy levels high. To maintain mental and physical freshness every day, we need to carve out time for these micro-moments of joy. By making a list of activities that bring us happiness and scheduling them randomly throughout the day, we create micro-recharge points. This practice helps sustain peak performance and ensures that our energy levels don't deplete.

These small, yet significant, moments are essential for renewing your energy to maintain both performance levels and happiness. These micro-enjoyable moments can be as varied as:

- **Listening to Music:**   Tune into your favourite songs or discover new ones to uplift your spirits.
- **Spending Time with Kids:**   Enjoy the innocence and joy children bring to any moment.
- **Rigorous Exercise:**   Engage in physical activity to release endorphins and boost your mood.
- **Reading:**   Dive into a chapter of a book or read for a few minutes to escape into another world.

- **Breathing Exercises or Yoga:**   Practice mindfulness to calm your mind and body.
- **Going for a Walk:**   Step outside to breathe fresh air and clear your mind.
- **Calling a Friend:**   Have a short, meaningful conversation to feel connected and supported.

Anything that allows you to take a break from a particular task and relax can serve as a micro-recharge point. By incorporating these activities, you ensure your energy levels remain high, helping you sustain your performance and happiness throughout the day.

So, make your list, sprinkle these joyful moments across your day and watch as your happiness and productivity soar!

> *"You cannot protect yourself from sadness*
> *without protecting yourself from Happiness."*
> —**Jonathan Safran Foer**

As they say, a change in activity is as good as a rest. True rest isn't merely taking a nap, binge-watching Netflix, or turning into a couch potato. Rest can be about engaging in something meaningful that rejuvenates you. Don't get me wrong—pursuing lofty goals sometimes means tackling tasks we don't particularly enjoy. However, our minds and bodies, much like machines, require regular maintenance and care.

It's essential to tackle the most challenging tasks of the day when our concentration levels are at their peak. This isn't right after a heavy meal or a particularly tough day. Take Jeff Bezos, for instance. As the CEO of Amazon, he describes his role as making tough and critical decisions. To optimise his performance, he schedules his most important meetings at 10 a.m. daily, when his energy levels are at their highest.

Bill Gates offers another excellent example of how simple activities can relax us. Despite his immense wealth, he continues to wash and dry his dishes every night. He finds this simple chore relaxing, helping him unwind before sleep.

If someone like Gates can find relaxation in such a humble task, surely we can all discover our micro-moments of joy. Identifying and indulging in small activities that bring us peace and relaxation can make a significant difference in our overall well-being.

GIVE MORE THAN WHAT YOU GET

One of the remarkable qualities that happy and successful people consistently exhibit is their commitment to giving more than they receive. This principle of generosity and altruism seems to be a cornerstone of their success and happiness.

Take, for instance, Dr. Bala Balachandran, the esteemed Dean of Great Lakes Institute of Management. Dr. Bala, or Uncle Bala, as we used to call him, embodies this quality to its fullest. Whenever someone seeks his assistance, he goes above and beyond to help. This characteristic was eloquently highlighted in a speech by his son, Sudhakar Balachandran, who credited his father's success to this very trait.

This concept is further explored in Adam Grant's insightful book, *Give and Take*. Grant, a renowned professor at the Wharton Business School, presents compelling research showing that people who prioritise giving tend to be more liked and, ultimately, more successful than their counterparts. His work substantiates the idea that generosity leads not only to personal satisfaction but also to professional success.

Moreover, the act of giving brings immense joy and fulfilment. Seeing the happiness and relief on others' faces can significantly boost our own sense of well-being. It reaffirms our belief in the power of altruism, creating a ripple effect of positivity and happiness.

In essence, giving more than you get is not just a path to success, but a profound way to enrich our lives and those of others. It strengthens our connections, builds trust, and fosters a sense of community, making the world a better place, one act of kindness at a time.

> ***"Three grand essentials to happiness in this life are something to do, something to love, and something to hope for."***
>
> **—Joseph Addison**

One common trait I've noticed among happy and successful people is their intrinsic drive to give more than they receive. This quality is not just about material generosity but extends to the way they interact with others, often with no expectation of return.

A beautiful illustration of this can be found in Dale Carnegie's classic book, *How to Win Friends and Influence People.* Carnegie recounts an incident where he approached a stranger and complimented his hairstyle. When sharing this story in one of his classes, a student asked, "But why did you do it? What did you want from him?" Carnegie, visibly upset by the question, simply replied, "I did not want anything from him. I just wanted the person to be happy."

This anecdote highlights a crucial aspect of genuine giving – doing it unconditionally. Carnegie had nothing to gain from this interaction; his sole intention was to bring a moment of happiness to another person. This mindset of giving without expecting anything in return is vital.

Giving goes beyond material possessions. One of the most profound forms of giving is sharing knowledge. The Bhagavad Gita emphasises that the highest form of giving is the imparting of wisdom. This philosophy is one of the motivations behind my writing. Having read many enlightening books, I feel compelled to share the knowledge I've gained with others, particularly on the topic of happiness, which has fascinated me for a long time.

For years, I've reflected on what makes people truly happy and wanted to share my insights to help others accelerate their own journeys towards happiness. Through this book, I hope to provide valuable reflections and knowledge that can benefit readers, fostering a deeper understanding and a more fulfilling path to joy.

*"The happiness which is lacking makes
one think even the happiness one has is Unbearable."*
—Joseph Roux

BALANCING EXTRINSIC AND INTRINSIC MOTIVATION

One of the most intriguing and enduring debates revolves around the sources of our happiness. Is it the physical or material pleasures that bring us joy, or is it the intrinsic motivations driven by our sense of worth and fulfilment? This question remains as relevant today as ever, sparking diverse opinions and thoughtful discussions.

Philosophical and spiritual texts often lean towards the importance of intrinsic motivation. They suggest that true contentment comes from within, stemming from our sense of purpose and inner peace. However, this perspective is frequently countered by the voices of those who have achieved great wealth and success. They might argue, "Why not become rich first and then decide if you don't need external motivation to stay happy?"

Sudha Murthy, a renowned philanthropist, addressed this duality brilliantly in one of her speeches. When asked if it felt good to be rich, she candidly replied, "Actually, being rich is not so bad." Her wealth allows her to invest in meaningful projects and contribute to society in ways that would not be possible if she were poor. For her, being rich enhances the joy of giving, demonstrating that wealth can indeed complement intrinsic motivations.

This brings us to a nuanced understanding: the key to happiness may not lie exclusively in either extrinsic or intrinsic motivations, but in a delicate balance between the 2. Different tasks and contexts may require different sources of motivation. For instance, extrinsic rewards might drive us to achieve certain goals, while intrinsic satisfaction keeps us passionate and fulfilled in our pursuits.

Thus, the challenge and the skill lie in knowing how to balance these motivations effectively. By understanding when to draw on external incentives and when to nurture our inner drives, we can navigate our lives more joyfully and meaningfully. In essence, a harmonious blend of both extrinsic and intrinsic motivation might be the true secret to lasting happiness and fulfilment.

In fields where physical performance or repetitive tasks are key, extrinsic motivation often proves to be a more effective driver than intrinsic motivation. For example, athletes or professionals engaged in physical labour benefit greatly from an extrinsic drive to excel (e.g. awards or competitive events like the Olympics), rather than intrinsic rewards. However, when tasks demand creativity and people management skills, intrinsic motivation again shows its superiority. Research consistently highlights that the satisfaction and passion from within fuel better performance in such areas.

Understanding when to apply extrinsic motivation is crucial. For tasks requiring physical ability, setting clear goals and milestones is beneficial. Take fitness, for instance—setting specific milestones and a structured plan can significantly enhance your chances of achieving optimal health and fitness.

On the other hand, if your pursuit involves complex decisions or entrepreneurial endeavours where success is uncertain, discovering your purpose becomes paramount. This sense of meaning and empowerment provides the missionary zeal needed to drive yourself forward. When your work aligns with your intrinsic values, the motivation to excel comes naturally.

It's important to recognise that the balance between intrinsic and extrinsic motivation also depends on the life cycle of the task. At the outset, intrinsic motivation is essential. When starting an activity, the purpose may not be clear, and rigid plans or milestones may hinder progress. In these initial stages, a deep, internal drive can provide the necessary direction and adaptability to navigate through uncertainties.

Embarking on an entrepreneurial journey can be filled with uncertainty and unforeseen challenges. As Prof. Clayton Christensen aptly puts it, "It is a very bad idea for an entrepreneur who has just started on his journey and new business to establish very clear goals, significant milestones, and very clear business plans." This is because the chances are very high that the person is going to miss his projections. At the start of the entrepreneurial journey, things are often so unclear that it is nearly impossible to set a goal or a revenue target and achieve it.

In the beginning, it's crucial to be intrinsically motivated. This phase involves complex decision-making and learning the ropes, while juggling multiple tasks simultaneously. Intrinsic motivation, driven by personal satisfaction and a sense of accomplishment, can help navigate this uncertainty.

As progress is made, it becomes important to start incorporating extrinsic motivation to measure success against industry standards. This comparison helps determine if we are progressing well and meeting the benchmarks considered best in class.

This balance is not just important for individual entrepreneurs, but also for managers and team leaders. When leading a team that is just getting started, intrinsic motivation can drive better performance. However, as the team moves into more operational tasks or further down the product life cycle, introducing structured processes can reduce anxiety and enable the team to deliver superior results.

Ultimately, the key to a happy and fruitful life lies in learning to balance extrinsic and intrinsic motivation factors. This balance should depend on the context and the stage of the work being done. By understanding when to leverage each type of motivation, individuals and teams can achieve greater success and satisfaction in their endeavours.

"You can't be happy unless you're unhappy Sometimes."
—Lauren Oliver

WORK FOR WORK'S SAKE

Our scripture, the Bhagavad Gita, extensively discusses karma yoga. On the battlefield, Lord Krishna engages in a lengthy conversation with Arjuna, who is uncertain about whether to fight or not. Lord Krishna emphasises, "You are a Kshatriya. Focus on the work, not the results." This is encapsulated in the famous saying:

Karmanye Vadhikaraste, Ma Phaleshou Kada Chana
Ma Karma Phala Hetur Bhurmatey, Sangostva Akarmani

In simple terms, this means:

You have the right to perform your prescribed duty, but you are not entitled to the fruits of your actions.

The principle is clear: Lord Krishna advises Arjuna to concentrate on the task at hand without worrying about the results. This provides an essential clue for us in our quest for happiness.

A crucial trait of a person who finds true happiness is one who does not expect rewards but performs their work with utmost dedication and perfection. When we work for the sake of work itself, certain characteristics confirm that we are doing it correctly and possess a genuine love for the work we do.

The first and most important quality to develop is the ability to quiet the mind. When we work merely for the sake of working, our mind can achieve a certain state of calmness. However, if we analyse deeply, we realise that our mind is constantly chattering. Research indicates that we experience around 60,000 thoughts every day, which is the average number of thoughts.

With so many thoughts, our mind is perpetually active, whether it's describing a current situation, comparing it to the past, or anticipating the future. Often, our mind is preoccupied with various situations or problems we face, leading to constant mental chatter. Therefore, the most crucial quality we need to cultivate is the ability to quieten the mind.

> *"As people spin faster and faster in the pursuit of merely personal happiness, they become exhausted in the futile effort of chasing themselves."*
> **—Andrew Delbanco**

And the only way to quiet the mind is to be fully absorbed in the task at hand.

For example, when we play a game of chess that we love, we often lose track of time, unaware of how many hours have passed. This happens because our mind is completely absorbed in the task, preventing any train of thoughts from disturbing us.

Some might argue that such tranquillity can also be achieved through a vacation or a relaxing activity, like playing chess. While these activities are indeed important for happiness and relaxation, there's a crucial difference to consider.

Although happiness and relaxation are vital, it is equally important to find meaning in the work we do. When our work benefits others or contributes positively to the world, it provides a sense of heightened satisfaction that self-centred or purely self-beneficial work cannot offer. Engaging in meaningful work not only quiets the mind but also enriches our lives, creating a profound sense of purpose and fulfilment.

To illustrate, think about someone dedicating their time to volunteer work. The joy and contentment they feel stem not just from the act of helping, but from knowing that their efforts make a difference in someone else's life. This sense of purpose quiets the mind and brings inner peace in a way that mere relaxation cannot.

In essence, to achieve a tranquil mind, we must immerse ourselves fully in our tasks, especially those that hold meaning and purpose. This dual approach of finding joy in our work and knowing it benefits others can lead to a deeper, more satisfying form of inner calm.

For this, I would like to draw your attention to a profound example of commitment: the Father of our nation, Mahatma Gandhi. He dedicated his life to India's freedom struggle, consistently prioritising his work, goals, and mission over personal and worldly concerns.

Gandhi's unwavering focus on his mission is a testament to the power of meaningful work. He found deep purpose in his efforts to free India from colonial rule, and this purpose drove him to remain steadfast in the face of immense challenges. His ability to stay fully absorbed in his mission not only quieted his mind but also inspired millions to join his cause.

Gandhi's life teaches us that when we commit ourselves to a cause greater than ourselves, we can achieve extraordinary levels of dedication and tranquillity. His work was not for personal gain, but for the benefit of an entire nation, illustrating how meaningful work can bring about profound personal satisfaction and a sense of peace.

In our own lives, we may not face the same monumental challenges, but we can still draw inspiration from Gandhi's example. By seeking out and dedicating ourselves to work that benefits others and aligns with our values, we can achieve a similar state of inner calm and fulfilment. Whether it's through our professional endeavours, volunteer activities, or personal projects, finding meaning in what we do is key to quieting the mind and living a more satisfying life.

"To have great happiness, you have to experience great pain and unhappiness – otherwise, how would you know when you're happy?"

—Leslie Caron

ABILITY TO BREAK IT DOWN

The other day, a lightbulb went out in my kitchen. I grabbed a chair and a new bulb, ready to fix it quickly. But no matter how hard I twisted, the old bulb wouldn't budge. After several minutes of struggle and near falls, I sat down, frustrated. That's when I noticed—there were screws on the fixture I hadn't seen. The solution wasn't brute force; it was a simple first step I'd overlooked. Just like in life, problems often seem huge until we break them down into smaller, manageable tasks.

One of the most valuable qualities we can cultivate for a fulfilling and content life is our ability to break down the problems we face. Think about it: what exactly makes a problem hard? A hard problem is simply one that hasn't yet been dissected into its smaller, manageable parts. When a problem remains whole, it looms large and intimidating, overwhelming us.

We often feel anxious when confronting such problems because we lack a clear sense of direction or certainty. The initial stage, before a problem is broken down, is where most of our stress originates. However, if we take the time to deconstruct a problem into its constituent parts and examine them closely, we begin to see the path forward.

Each part of a problem can be addressed individually. It's important to recognise that we may not have the ability to solve every part on our own. This is where we can leverage the expertise of others. We might recruit a specialist, ask a friend for advice, or seek support from family members to help tackle different aspects of the problem.

The key is to match our skills to the components of the problem we can handle and to be realistic about the time required to resolve each part. Breaking down a hard problem into smaller, manageable pieces not only makes it less daunting, but also empowers us to take decisive, effective action. By approaching problems in this methodical way, we can navigate challenges with greater confidence and ultimately achieve a sense of satisfaction and happiness.

When I embarked on writing this book, I knew from the start that it needed to be structured into 7 chapters. Breaking it down this way allowed me to plan my writing schedule effectively, deciding exactly how many hours a day I needed to dedicate to the task. This method of tackling the book in smaller sections not only made the project more manageable but also significantly reduced my anxiety.

Similarly, when we take any problem and break it down into smaller, manageable pieces, we make the entire process smoother and less stressful. This approach also allows us to pace ourselves. Life, as they say, is not a sprint but a marathon. We need to pace ourselves according to our skills and prepare to solve each component of the larger problem we face.

Breaking down problems is crucial because it emboldens us to accept difficult challenges and handle them effectively. This method helps us to tackle problems that have a significant impact, while maintaining our composure and equilibrium, preventing us from feeling overwhelmed.

When we manage to control our minds in this way, our intellectual and creative capabilities can reach their maximum potential. By taking a step-by-step approach, we can navigate through challenges more effectively, leading to greater satisfaction and success.

> *"There are 2 things to aim at in life: first,*
> *to get what you want; and after that, to enjoy it.*
> *Only the wisest of mankind achieve the second."*
> **—Logan Pearsall Smith**

WORK FOR YOURSELF

Another essential quality we must develop is to stop seeking approval from others for the work we plan to do. As mentioned earlier, seeking a happy life involves understanding what happiness means for us individually.

How to Redefine Happiness?

Our definition of happiness can be vastly different from someone else's. As long as we understand our own definition of happiness, we should not let others dictate how we should be happy.

Often, I notice many people constantly seek approval from others. They fail to realise that every time they seek validation, they give the outside world the power to control them. Gradually, they become slaves to another person's compliments or approvals.

When we become answerable only to ourselves, it creates a tremendous amount of freedom, allowing us to live life on our terms. However, this newfound freedom comes with responsibility. The moment we stop seeking approval from others, we must become accountable for our actions and conduct.

Therefore, when we stop seeking approval from others, we must strive for perfection in our tasks. This self-driven pursuit of excellence is what will ultimately lead us to true fulfilment and happiness.

We must focus on continuous improvement, aiming to achieve world-class standards and set benchmarks. We need to be leaders in our chosen field. As Michael Jordan aptly puts it, "Let the game do the talking."

Just as we should avoid seeking approval from others, we must also refrain from being judgemental and blaming others. Excuses for our current life situation are counterproductive. Often, people perceive their circumstances as a result of external influences. However, even if external factors are at play, the only thing we can control is our behaviour and reaction.

Instead of complaining and generating negative energy for ourselves, our team, and those around us, we should reflect and ask ourselves, "What do we need to do to change the situation?" Remember, when you point a finger at someone else, 4 fingers point back at you. We need to look inward and determine what actions we can take, rather than wasting time complaining about the world.

The world is not out to tease us; it is there for us to take charge, work harder, and do better. It won't always align with our thoughts and imagination, but that's no excuse to give up.

When we stop seeking approval and take responsibility for our actions, we embark on the path to true happiness. By focusing on what we can control and striving for excellence, we not only improve ourselves, but also inspire those around us.

> *"He who lives in harmony with himself,*
> *lives in harmony with the Universe."*
>
> —Marcus Aurelius

KEY VALUES FOR A FULFILLING AND ENRICHING LIFE

True fulfilment arises not from transient pleasures, but from a deeper, more holistic development of purpose and value creation.

Key values mentioned in Bhagavad Gita verse 16.3.1 should be embodied in our daily lives. This final section is not a mere translation of the verse, but more a reflection on how best to use timeless wisdom to build a moral compass that can guide our actions.

- **Fearlessness (Lack of Ignorance)**
  Fearlessness stems from knowledge and the absence of ignorance. It is not merely the absence of fear, but a state of profound awareness. If you have seen the movie 300, you would remember the famous line where the lone boy, King Leonidus, faces the wolf in the forest. 'It is not fear that grips him, but a heightened sense of things!'
  By seeking truth and understanding, individuals can overcome the limitations imposed by ignorance. Embracing fearlessness means facing challenges with courage and clarity, knowing that each experience is a step towards greater wisdom and not being worried about failures that are bound to arise during our journey!

- **Purity of Heart (Righteousness)**
  Purity of heart involves having pure motives and intentions. It is about being righteous in our actions and thoughts.
  In an organisational context, it will be about creating impact or delivering value to clients and holding people accountable to high standards to deliver on this goal. In a personal context, having the right long-term goal and

a willingness to make short-term sacrifices, or having difficult conversations when the need arises. It could be about speaking the truth, even if unpopular, to do the right thing!

When our hearts are pure, we act with integrity and honesty, ensuring that our deeds align with our moral and ethical values. This purity fosters trust and respect in our relationships and contributes to a peaceful mind.

The purity of heat is also linked with fear. When we act without the right motive, then we deep down know what we are doing is wrong, leading to fear! But with the right intention, even people who are initially ignorant will eventually realise our true motives and support us.

- **Charity (Oneness and Abundance)**

Charity is the expression of recognising oneness with others. It is the act of giving selflessly, knowing that abundance flows from a generous heart.

In an organisational context, it could be as simple as helping someone without expecting anything in return. On the personal front, it could be just expressing unconditional love and being ready to serve before being asked to!

Charity is not limited to material wealth but also includes giving time, love and compassion. It promotes a sense of community and interconnectedness, enriching both the giver and the receiver.

- **Self-Control (Conservation of Energy)**

Practising self-control means managing desires and impulses effectively.

In an organisational context, it could be avoidance of reacting to someone who is outright rude to us or disrespects us—having the courage later to confront the individual to give constructive feedback so that they do not repeat this behaviour or choose their words more carefully! On the personal front, it could be just letting it go. Things will not go as per our plan, and sometimes we cannot do anything about it. So just chill and focus on impactful things and where we can exercise more control.

By conserving our energy and focusing it on productive and meaningful pursuits, we can achieve greater clarity and purpose. Self-control also aids in maintaining physical and mental health, contributing to overall well-being.

- **Straightforwardness and Simplicity**
  Straightforwardness involves being honest and transparent in our dealings. Simplicity is about living a life free from deceit and complexity.

  Calling a spade a spade, just giving honest feedback when asked, keeping things simple, and acting with no hidden agenda are some of the values that will lead to a much richer life, win trust, and build deep relationships.

  Embracing these qualities fosters authenticity and builds trust in relationships, creating a harmonious environment.

- **Non-violence and Truthfulness**
  Nonviolence means abstaining from causing harm, both physically and emotionally.

  I don't understand why people act rudely. They perhaps do this to feel important, not realising that their rudeness will only lead to alienation.

  Truthfulness is about being sincere and honest in our communication. These values promote peace and trust, reducing conflicts and fostering harmonious interactions.

- **Freedom from Anger and Renunciation**
  Freedom from anger involves not letting anger overwhelm us. It requires patience and understanding. Renunciation is about letting go of attachments and maintaining an even temper. These values help in achieving inner peace and balance.

- **Tranquillity and Aversion to Fault-finding**
  Tranquillity is maintaining balance and calmness in all situations. Aversion to fault-finding means controlling the urge to criticise others. These values promote inner peace and positive relationships.

- **Compassion and Freedom from Covetousness**
  Compassion involves being tolerant of others' imperfections and showing kindness. Freedom from covetousness means not being greedy and being content with what we have. These values foster empathy and satisfaction.

- **Gentleness, Modesty and Steady Determination**
  Gentleness and modesty reflect the grace and humility in one's conduct. Steady determination involves being resolute and unwavering in our goals. These values contribute to personal growth and respect in society.

- **Vigour, Forgiveness and Fortitude**
  Vigour is the inner glow and joy that comes from living a purpose-driven life. Forgiveness involves letting go of grudges, and fortitude is the faith and strength to persevere. These values enhance resilience and positivity.

- **Cleanliness and Freedom from Hatred**
  Cleanliness is maintaining purity in body and mind. Freedom from hatred means not harbouring ill feelings towards others. These values promote a healthy and harmonious life.

- **Absence of Over-Pride**
  The absence of over-pride involves humility and recognising the value of others. It means understanding that pride can lead to isolation and conflict, while humility fosters connection and mutual respect.

  By reflecting upon and incorporating these values into our lives, we can achieve a state of holistic fulfilment. The Bhagavad Gita's timeless wisdom provides a guiding light, helping us navigate the complexities of life with grace, purpose and joy.

CONCLUSION

In Chapter 7, we delved into various qualities essential for achieving inner peace and happiness. Understanding what happiness means to each of us individually sets the foundation for a fulfilling life. Recognising different types of happiness, from sensory pleasures to profound inner peace, helps us appreciate the diverse ways in which joy can manifest. By writing down our goals, we align our daily actions with our long-term aspirations, fostering a sense of purpose and control. Developing strong habits, speaking up when necessary, seeking challenges, and giving more than we get, all contribute to a balanced and content life. Moreover, finding meaning in our work and learning to break down complex problems are crucial for maintaining equilibrium and achieving success. Finally, working for our own satisfaction rather than seeking external approval empowers us to live authentically and joyfully. Together, these qualities form a comprehensive checklist for nurturing inner peace and happiness, guiding us toward a fulfilling and joyful life.

KEY TAKEAWAYS

1. **Define Your Happiness:** Understanding what happiness means to you is the first step towards a fulfilling life. This definition is personal and unique to each individual.

2. **Recognise Different Types of Happiness:** Happiness can come from sensory pleasures, achievements, relationships, and inner peace. Appreciating these different forms helps us find joy in various aspects of life.

3. **Write Down Your Goals:** Setting and documenting goals provides clarity and motivation, aligning daily actions with long-term aspirations.

4. **Develop Strong Habits:** Building and sticking to positive habits enhances productivity, reduces stress and fosters a sense of accomplishment.

5. **Speak Up Wisely:** Use the four filters—truth, gentleness, intention, and necessity—before speaking. This ensures effective and considerate communication.

6. **Seek Challenges:** Embrace new challenges to learn and grow. Continuous self-improvement leads to greater fulfilment.

7. **Give More Than You Get:** Generosity and altruism not only benefit others, but also bring immense joy and satisfaction to the giver.

8. **Find Meaning in Your Work:** Engaging in work that benefits others and aligns with your values brings a deeper sense of purpose and tranquility.

9. **Break Down Problems:** Deconstructing complex issues into manageable parts makes them less daunting and more solvable.

10. **Work for Yourself:** Stop seeking external approval and take responsibility for your actions. Striving for personal excellence leads to true happiness.

These key takeaways serve as a guide to cultivating a balanced, joyful and meaningful life.

> *"The happiness of your life depends*
> *upon the quality of your thoughts."*
>
> **—Marcus Aurelius**

Closing Thoughts

As we come to the end of this journey through *The Happiness Flywheel*, I hope the pages you've turned have brought clarity, inspiration, and a sense of direction. My purpose in writing this book was to help you find meaning and experience true happiness in your life. Drawing from academic research, personal experience, and spiritual texts, I have attempted to create a blueprint that guides you toward a deeper, more comprehensible understanding of happiness.

Every human being embarks on a quest for happiness from the moment they are born. Some achieve it, while others continue their search throughout their lives. However, one thing is clear: those who attain happiness also create a more meaningful impact, not only in their own lives, but in the lives of their families, communities, and beyond.

The essence of this book lies in its simplicity and coherence. I have strived to present complex concepts in an understandable way, ensuring that every reader can grasp the principles and apply them to their daily lives.

THE BLUEPRINT FOR HAPPINESS

In this book, we've explored various facets of happiness, recognising that it is a multi-dimensional pursuit. Here's a brief recap of the roadmap we've journeyed together:

CHAPTER 1

Finding Your Flow and Doing Your Duty

We started with the importance of discovering your purpose and achieving a state of flow. Engaging in meaningful activities and setting specific goals can lead to a consistent experience of happiness.

CHAPTER 2

Developing the Right Mindset

We delved into the necessity of maintaining the right attitude and mindset. The ends don't justify the means; it's crucial to pursue goals without sacrificing inner peace and joy.

CHAPTER 3

Avoiding Practices That Derail Happiness

We discussed the behaviours that can hinder happiness and how to consciously avoid them. Recognising and eliminating these detrimental practices can help maintain a positive and fulfilling journey.

CHAPTER 4

Building Strong Relationships

We emphasised the importance of nurturing strong relationships. Success is not a solitary journey, and having a supportive network amplifies the sense of accomplishment and happiness.

CHAPTER 5

Developing Detachment and Resilience

We explored strategies to build resilience and a sense of detachment. These qualities are essential for navigating life's challenges without compromising inner peace and well-being.

CHAPTER 6

Finding Balance and Peace

We focused on creating a resilient framework to maintain peace of mind. Achieving higher levels of happiness involves attaining a state of tranquillity, even in adversity.

CHAPTER 7

Cultivating Qualities That Define a Happy Life

Finally, we identified the qualities that define a happy life, such as fearlessness, honesty, and straightforwardness. These attributes support the quest for genuine happiness and lasting fulfilment.

As you reflect on the insights and tools presented in this book, I encourage you to try out the ideas that resonate with your life. Experiment with the concepts, integrate them into your daily routine, and observe the transformation they bring. Not every idea may directly apply to you, and that's perfectly fine. Selectively embrace the concepts that align with your path and leave behind what doesn't resonate.

The pursuit of happiness is a universal journey, and I hope this book has provided you with a practical guide to navigate it. By fostering happiness and well-being, you can lead a contented life filled with energy and inner peace. May this journey of self-discovery lead you to the pinnacle of happiness, allowing you to redeem it and sustain it throughout your life.

Thank you for being a part of this exploration. I wish you all the best in your continued search for happiness and fulfilment.

> *"Happiness is not a state to arrive at,*
> *but a manner of traveling."*
>
> —Margaret Lee Runbeck

EPILOGUE: A JOURNEY OF GRATITUDE

As we reach the final pages of this book, I want to extend my deepest gratitude to you—the reader. Thank you for investing your time in absorbing the insights that I have carefully curated over the years, drawing from my corporate experiences, my academic journey, and the profound teachings of the Bhagavad Gita and other spiritual texts. This book was not just written to inform but to serve as a toolkit that you can return to at different stages of your life, depending on the challenges and opportunities you encounter.

To the younger audience, for whom this book was particularly intended, I hope it has sparked reflection and inspired you to become not only successful professionals but also individuals of integrity, empathy, and purpose. As you continue your journey, may you strive to be good corporate citizens, supportive family members, and, above all, great human beings—setting an example for others to follow.

I am deeply grateful to the mentors and leaders who have shaped my thinking and supported me in crafting this work. My teachers from IIM Ahmedabad, and those from MIT, Columbia Business School, INSEAD, ISB, Great Lakes, and Anna University, all played a critical role in shaping my worldview, particularly in emphasizing the importance of research, reflection, and continual learning. I am also indebted to my colleagues—leaders like Mohit Joshi, Richard Lobo, S. Mahalingam, Dilip Keshu, Pratik Pal, Ananth Krishnan, Rajani Seshadri, PR Krishnan, Amit Bhalla, Damodar Padhi, Arun Nair, Jayaram Rajaram, Ganapathy S, Dr. Mohan Kancharla, and many others—who took the time to review this book and provide invaluable feedback.

Lastly, I want to acknowledge my family, whose unwavering support during the five-year journey of writing this book, especially through the trials of the COVID-19 pandemic, gave me the strength to complete it. This book stands as a testament to their love and encouragement.

I look forward to hearing your thoughts, reflections, and stories. Please feel free to write to me at krishnan.c.a2004@ gmail.com. Let us continue this dialogue as we explore the vast and ever-evolving journey toward happiness and fulfillment.

Thank you for being part of this journey with me. Wishing you all the best in your pursuit of happiness, purpose, and impact.

Bibliography and Literature Review

This section of my book delves into the rigorous academic research underpinning the key concepts discussed. I have meticulously reviewed academic articles that reference these concepts, ensuring that my interpretations are grounded in empirical evidence. However, the dense nature of these academic journals can be challenging for the general reader to navigate. My goal with this book is to simplify these concepts, providing a clear roadmap and blueprint for those seeking happiness, while ensuring that my conclusions are supported by solid academic research.

This section will serve as a gateway to deeper exploration for those with a more scholarly interest. You will find references to pivotal studies, such as the Marshmallow Experiment, and other influential papers. This approach ensures that, while the book remains accessible, it also offers a pathway for readers to engage with the underlying academic research.

CHAPTER 1
Literature Review

The quest for purpose in life is a fundamental human endeavour, deeply intertwined with psychological well-being and overall life satisfaction. This literature review examines various perspectives on this topic, drawing from key academic sources, to compare and contrast different viewpoints.

Kendall Cotton Bronk (2014) emphasises the significance of having a life purpose for optimal youth development. Bronk posits that a clear sense of purpose is crucial for young people as it guides their choices and helps them navigate life's challenges. She highlights that purpose provides a framework for setting and achieving goals, which, in turn, fosters resilience and a sense of fulfilment (Bronk, 2014). This perspective aligns with the broader positive psychology movement, which stresses the importance of purpose in achieving a well-rounded and fulfilling life (Seligman & Csikszentmihalyi, 2000).

Similarly, Michaéla C. Schippers and Niklas Ziegler (2019) introduce the concept of "life crafting" as a method for finding purpose. Their approach involves structured interventions that help individuals reflect on their values, passions, and goals. Schippers and Ziegler argue that such interventions can enhance an individual's sense of control and direction in life, thereby promoting happiness and well-being (Schippers & Ziegler, 2019). This method is rooted in the positive psychology framework and resonates with Bronk's emphasis on goal-setting and personal growth.

William Damon, Jenni Menon, and Kendall Cotton Bronk (2003) explore the development of purpose during adolescence, highlighting the formative nature of these years. They argue that adolescents who develop a clear sense of purpose are better equipped to handle life's transitions and are more likely to experience psychological well-being. This developmental perspective underscores the importance of early interventions to help young people discover and cultivate their life purposes (Damon, Menon, & Bronk, 2003).

In contrast, Ryff and Keyes (1995) approach the topic from the angle of psychological well-being, identifying purpose as one of 6 core dimensions that contribute to a person's overall sense of wellness. They argue that having a purpose in life is essential for achieving high levels of psychological well-being and life satisfaction. Ryff and Keyes' model is comprehensive, integrating purpose with other factors such as self-acceptance, positive relationships, and personal growth, thus providing a holistic view of well-being (Ryff & Keyes, 1995).

Hill et al. (2010) examine the long-term effects of purpose developed during college on adult well-being. They find that individuals who cultivate a sense of purpose in their collegiate years tend to experience higher levels of well-being in adulthood. This longitudinal perspective highlights the enduring impact of purpose on life satisfaction and underscores the importance of fostering purpose early in life (Hill et al., 2010).

Comparing these perspectives reveals both commonalities and differences. Most notably, there is a consensus on the critical role of purpose in achieving psychological well-being and life satisfaction. Bronk (2014) and Schippers & Ziegler (2019) emphasise the developmental and interventionist approaches, suggesting structured methods to help individuals find and cultivate their purpose. On the other hand, Ryff & Keyes (1995) and Hill et al. (2010) offer broader frameworks that integrate purpose with other dimensions of well-being and highlight its long-term benefits.

These insights provide valuable guidance for both individuals seeking to find their purpose and practitioners aiming to support them in this quest.

Bibliography

These references provide a comprehensive overview of the importance of finding purpose in life and how it relates to psychological well-being and development.

- Bronk, K.C., 2014. Purpose in Life: A Critical Component of Optimal Youth Development. Dordrecht: Springer. This book explores the development of life purposes in youth and highlights how having a purpose is essential for optimal development across the lifespan.

- Damon, W., Menon, J., & Bronk, K.C., 2003. The development of purpose during adolescence. Applied Developmental Science, 7(3), pp. 119-128. doi: 10.1207/S1532480XADS0703_2. This paper discusses how adolescents develop a sense of purpose and its implications for their overall development.
- Schippers, M.C., & Ziegler, N., 2019. Life Crafting as a Way to Find Purpose and Meaning in Life. Frontiers in Psychology, 10, Article 2778. doi: 10.3389/fpsyg.2019.02778. This article presents a life-crafting intervention as a structured approach to help individuals find purpose and meaning in their lives.
- Hill, P.L., Burrow, A.L., Brandenberger, J.W., Lapsley, D.K. & Quaranto, J.C., 2010. Collegiate purpose orientations and well-being in adulthood. Journal of Applied Developmental Psychology, 31(3), pp. 173-179. doi:10.1016/j.appdev.2009.12.001. This study examines how purpose orientations developed during college can impact well-being in adulthood.
- Ryff, C.D., & Keyes, C.L.M., 1995. The structure of psychological well-being revisited. Journal of Personality and Social Psychology, 69(4), pp. 719-727. doi: 10.1037/0022-3514.69.4.719. This foundational paper on psychological well-being includes discussions on the role of purpose in achieving overall life satisfaction.

CHAPTER 2
Literature Review

The literature on developing the right attitude for success and happiness is rich and multifaceted, drawing on various psychological theories and empirical studies.

Blazar and Kraft (2017) explore the impact of teachers on students' attitudes and behaviours, emphasising the role of effective teaching in fostering positive student outcomes. Their study highlights the significant influence of teachers in shaping students' attitudes towards learning and their overall academic behaviours. This perspective underscores the importance of the educational environment in cultivating a positive mindset, suggesting that external influences play a critical role in the development of attitudes that lead to success and happiness.

In contrast, Rajasekhar et al. (2022) focus on the role of spirituality, gratitude, and forgiveness in influencing happiness and academic performance. They propose that these intrinsic factors, mediated by happiness, significantly contribute to students' academic success. This study supports the idea that internal personal qualities and spiritual well-being are crucial for achieving happiness and success, presenting a more intrinsic approach compared to Blazar and Kraft's emphasis on external factors.

Lyubomirsky, King, and Diener (2005) provide a comprehensive overview of the benefits of positive affect, asserting that happiness leads to success across various life domains. Their research supports a bidirectional relationship where happiness not only results from success but also contributes to it. This aligns with Fredrickson's (2004) broaden-and-build theory, which posits that positive emotions expand an individual's thought-action repertoire, thereby building lasting personal resources. Both Lyubomirsky et al. and Fredrickson advocate for the proactive cultivation of positive emotions as a pathway to success and fulfilment, emphasising an intrinsic, emotion-based mechanism for achieving happiness.

Seligman and Csikszentmihalyi (2000) introduce the concept of positive psychology, which seeks to shift the focus from pathology to strengths and virtues that enable individuals and communities to thrive. They highlight the importance of fostering positive experiences, traits, and institutions, thereby advocating for a holistic approach to happiness that encompasses both individual and collective well-being. This perspective integrates both internal and external factors, suggesting a more balanced approach to developing the right attitude for success.

In synthesising these perspectives, several key themes emerge. Firstly, the role of intrinsic factors such as positive emotions, spirituality, gratitude, and forgiveness is highlighted by Rajasekhar et al. (2022), Lyubomirsky et al. (2005), and Fredrickson (2004). These studies collectively emphasise the importance of cultivating internal states of well-being as foundational to achieving success and happiness. Secondly, the impact of external influences, particularly in educational settings, is underscored by Blazar and Kraft (2017), who highlight the critical role of effective teaching in shaping positive student outcomes.

A notable contrast exists between the intrinsic focus of Rajasekhar et al. and Fredrickson, and the more extrinsic emphasis of Blazar and Kraft. However, Seligman and Csikszentmihalyi (2000) bridge this divide by advocating for a comprehensive approach that integrates both internal strengths and external support systems.

By integrating these diverse perspectives, a more holistic understanding of the pathways to success and happiness can be achieved.

Bibliography

These references provide further reading on the psychological and educational impacts of maintaining a positive attitude and cultivating the right mindset for success and happiness.

- Blazar, D., & Kraft, M.A. (2017). Teacher and Teaching Effects on Students' Attitudes and Behaviors. Educational Evaluation and Policy Analysis, 39(1), pp. 146-170.
- Rajasekhar, D., Singh, S., Ribeiro, N., & Gomes, D. R. (2022). Does Spirituality Influence Happiness and Academic Performance? Religions, 13(7), 617.

- Lyubomirsky, S., King, L., & Diener, E. (2005). The Benefits of Frequent Positive Affect: Does Happiness Lead to Success? Psychological Bulletin, 131(6), pp. 803-855.
- Seligman, M.E.P. & Csikszentmihalyi, M. (2000). Positive Psychology: An Introduction. American Psychologist, 55(1), pp. 5-14.
- Fredrickson, B.L. (2004). The Broaden-and-Build Theory of Positive Emotions. Philosophical Transactions of the Royal Society B: Biological Sciences, 359(1449), pp. 1367-1377.

CHAPTER 3
Literature Review

The concept of delayed gratification has been extensively studied, with numerous researchers contributing to our understanding of its implications for cognitive development, academic performance, and overall well-being. This literature review synthesises findings from several key studies, highlighting both converging and diverging perspectives on the significance of delayed gratification.

Mischel, Shoda, and Rodriguez's (1989) seminal work on the delay of gratification in children, commonly known as the Marshmallow Test, established the foundational understanding that the ability to delay gratification is a predictor of future success. Their research demonstrated that children who could wait longer for a larger reward tended to have better life outcomes, including higher academic achievement and better emotional regulation. This study laid the groundwork for subsequent research into the cognitive and behavioural aspects of delayed gratification.

Building on Mischel et al.'s findings, Saxler (2016) examined the Marshmallow Test in greater detail, focusing on independent rule compliance and the various modes of task termination. Saxler's analysis suggested that while the ability to delay gratification is crucial, the context in which it occurs, and the manner in which rules are followed also play significant roles in determining outcomes. This nuanced approach adds depth to our understanding by highlighting the complexity of the behaviours involved in the delay of gratification tasks.

Further exploring the cognitive mechanisms, Carlson and Meltzoff (2008) investigated the impact of bilingualism on executive functioning in young children. Their research found that bilingual children often exhibit superior executive functioning, including better inhibitory control, which is closely linked to delayed gratification. This study underscores the role of cognitive flexibility and control in enabling children to resist short-term temptations in favour of long-term rewards.

Watts, Duncan and Quan (2018) revisited the Marshmallow Test to assess its predictive validity across different contexts. They discovered that while the ability to delay gratification remains a valuable predictor of future success, its strength is moderated by various socio-economic factors. Their findings suggest that the context in which children develop and make decisions significantly influences their capacity for delayed gratification and its long-term benefits.

Duckworth and Seligman (2005) offered another perspective by emphasizing the importance of self-discipline over IQ in predicting academic performance. Their research indicated that self-discipline, a component of delayed gratification, is a more robust predictor of academic success than innate intelligence. This perspective aligns with Mischel et al.'s conclusions but extends the discussion to emphasize the critical role of self-regulatory skills in academic achievement.

Schlam et al. (2013) extended the examination of delayed gratification to health outcomes, specifically body mass index (BMI). Their longitudinal study found that preschoolers' ability to delay gratification predicted their BMI, 30 years later, suggesting that self-regulatory skills developed early in life have long-lasting health implications. This study adds a valuable dimension to the discussion by linking cognitive and behavioural traits to physical health outcomes.

Petersen et al. (2016) focused on the development of inhibitory control, a key component of delayed gratification. Their work highlighted the challenges of measuring this construct over time and emphasised the importance of understanding the developmental trajectory of self-regulatory skills. Their research supports the idea that enhancing inhibitory control can significantly improve children's capacity for delayed gratification.

Finally, Miller and Wallis (2015) explored the neural underpinnings of delayed gratification, identifying specific prefrontal regions involved in executive function and inter-temporal decision-making. Their findings suggest that the ability to delay gratification is not only a behavioural phenomenon but also deeply rooted in the brain's structure and function. This neuroscientific perspective provides a biological basis for the cognitive and behavioural observations made by other researchers.

Together, these studies underscore the critical role of self-regulatory skills in achieving success and well-being across the lifespan.

Bibliography

These references provide a comprehensive overview of the research on delayed gratification and its implications for various aspects of life, including academic performance, health and overall well-being.

- Mischel, W., Shoda, Y., & Rodriguez, M. L. (1989). "Delay of gratification in children." Science, 244(4907), 933-938.
- Saxler, P. K. (2016). "The Marshmallow Test: Delay of Gratification and Independent Rule Compliance." Doctoral dissertation, Harvard Graduate School of Education.

- Carlson, S. M., & Meltzoff, A. N. (2008). "Bilingual experience and executive functioning in young children." Developmental Science, 11(2), 282-298.
- Watts, T. W., Duncan, G. J., & Quan, H. Z. (2018). "Revisiting the Marshmallow Test: A Conceptual Replication Investigating Links Between Early Delay of Gratification and Later Outcomes." Psychological Science, 29(7), 1159-1177.
- Duckworth, A. L., & Seligman, M. E. P. (2005). "Self-discipline outdoes IQ in predicting academic performance of adolescents." Psychological Science, 16(12), 939-944.
- Schlam, T. R., Wilson, N. L., Shoda, Y., Mischel, W., & Ayduk, O. (2013). "Preschoolers' delay of gratification predicts their body mass, 30 years later." The Journal of Pediatrics, 162(1), 90-93.
- Petersen, I. T., Hoyniak, C. P., McQuillan, M. E., Bates, J. E., & Staples, A. D. (2016). "Measuring the development of inhibitory control: The challenge of heterotypic continuity." Developmental Review, 40, 25-71.
- Miller, H. E., & Wallis, J. D. (2015), "Separate neural representations of prediction and outcome in dopamine neurons." Nature Neuroscience, 18(4), 512-518.

CHAPTER 4
Literature Review

The importance of social connections and their impact on well-being has been extensively studied, with various authors offering complementary, and sometimes contrasting, views on the subject.

Sandstrom and Dunn (2014) highlight the significant role of weak social ties in enhancing well-being. Their study suggests that even brief interactions with acquaintances or strangers can lead to increased happiness, underscoring the importance of both the quantity and quality of social connections. This perspective is valuable in understanding that meaningful social interactions are not limited to close relationships but can occur in everyday encounters, contributing to overall life satisfaction.

Reis and Clark (2013) provide a nuanced view by focusing on perceived partner responsiveness in close relationships. Their research indicates that moments of high responsiveness from partners are associated with greater feelings of connection and life satisfaction. This finding aligns with Sandstrom and Dunn (2014) by emphasizing the quality of interactions, but it specifically highlights the importance of responsiveness and mutual understanding within close relationships, suggesting that deeper, more emotionally resonant interactions may have a more substantial impact on well-being.

Cole and Capitanio (2014) offer a physiological perspective by examining how social connections influence immune function. Their study on rhesus monkeys demonstrates that strong social ties can enhance immune response and improve health outcomes, suggesting that the benefits of social connections extend beyond psychological well-being to physical health. This research complements the findings of Sandstrom and Dunn (2014) and Reis and Clark (2013) by providing a biological basis for the positive effects of social interactions, thus reinforcing the idea that social connections are vital for overall health.

Seppala, Rossomando, and Doty (2013) delve into the broader implications of social connection and compassion, highlighting their roles in promoting mental and physical health. They argue that individuals who feel more connected to others experience lower levels of anxiety and depression, higher self-esteem, and greater empathy. This view is consistent with Cole and Capitanio (2014) in linking social connections to improved health outcomes but extends the discussion to include emotional and psychological benefits, thereby offering a more holistic view of well-being.

Cacioppo and Cacioppo (2018) discuss the adverse effects of loneliness, noting that a lack of social connections can lead to significant declines in both physical and psychological health. Their research underscores the importance of maintaining strong social ties to mitigate these negative outcomes. This perspective contrasts with the more positive focus of Sandstrom and Dunn (2014) and Seppala et al. (2013) by highlighting the severe consequences of social isolation, thereby reinforcing the necessity of fostering social connections for overall health and happiness.

These studies collectively suggest that fostering social connections is essential for a fulfilling and healthy life.

Bibliography

- Sandstrom, G.M., & Dunn, E.W. (2014). "Social interactions and well-being: The surprising power of weak ties." Personality and Social Psychology Bulletin, 40(7), 910-922. This paper explores how even brief social interactions with acquaintances and strangers can enhance well-being, emphasising the importance of both quantity and quality of social connections.
- Reis, H.T., & Clark, M.S. (2013). "Responsiveness in relationships and well-being." In The Oxford Handbook of Close Relationships (pp. 400-423). Oxford University Press. This chapter discusses how perceived partner responsiveness in everyday interactions positively influences feelings of social connection, hope, and life satisfaction.
- Cole, S.W., & Capitanio, J.P. (2014). "Loneliness and immune function in rhesus monkeys." Proceedings of the National Academy of Sciences, 111(32), 10714-10719. This research highlights the physiological impacts of social connection, showing that strong social ties can improve immune function and overall health.

- Seppala, E., Rossomando, T., & Doty, J.R. (2013). "Social connection and compassion: Important predictors of health and well-being." Social Research: An International Quarterly, 80(2), 411-430. This study underscores the role of social connection and compassion in promoting physical and mental health, suggesting that fostering these qualities can lead to greater well-being.
- Cacioppo, J.T., & Cacioppo, S. (2018), "The growing problem of loneliness." The Lancet, 391(10119), 426. This article reviews the adverse effects of loneliness on health and well-being, highlighting the importance of maintaining social connections to mitigate these effects.

These references provide a solid foundation for understanding the critical role of social connections, effective communication and altruism in enhancing happiness and well-being.

CHAPTER 5
Literature Review

The concept of resilience has been extensively explored across various disciplines, offering diverse perspectives on its development, measurement and implications for well-being. This literature review examines and contrasts the views of several authors, providing a comprehensive understanding of resilience.

Fletcher and Sarkar (2013) present an integrative process model of resilience, emphasising the interaction between protective factors and metacognitions in producing adaptive responses to stressors. They argue that resilience is a dynamic process influenced by personal attributes and situational resources. Their model aligns with the work of Martin and Marsh (2006), who introduced the 5-C model of academic resilience, highlighting confidence, coordination, control, composure, and commitment as critical factors (Fletcher and Sarkar, 2013; Martin and Marsh, 2006).

Contrastingly, Dunn et al. (2018) focus on medical students' well-being, proposing a conceptual model where positive and negative inputs either replenish or drain an individual's coping reservoir. This model underscores the importance of both personal traits and environmental factors in fostering resilience, offering a more holistic view compared to Martin and Marsh's focus on individual capabilities (Dunn et al., 2018).

In the educational context, Leipold and Greve (2009) suggest that resilience combines coping and developmental processes. Their approach considers resilience as a bridge between managing stress and overall personal growth. This perspective is echoed by the OECD (2011), which defines resilience as positive adaptation across multiple domains, such as reading, mathematics, and science. This cross-domain approach contrasts with the single-domain focus seen in earlier resilience studies (Leipold and Greve, 2009, OECD, 2011).

Crawford et al. (2020) examine the impact of acute stressors, like the COVID-19 pandemic, on academic professionals. They highlight the chronic stressors faced by academics, such as manuscript rejections and negative teaching evaluations, emphasising the need for resilience in maintaining work-life balance and productivity. This study aligns with the broader view of resilience as a response to both acute and chronic stressors, integrating personal and professional challenges (Crawford et al., 2020).

Baek, Cho, and Koo (2009) discuss the environmental consequences of globalization, indirectly relating to resilience by examining how external, large-scale changes impact individual and community adaptability. Their country-specific analysis underscores the importance of contextual factors in shaping resilience, complementing the individual-focused models presented by other researchers (Baek, Cho, and Koo, 2009).

Lastly, Connor and Zhang (2006) focus on the measurement of resilience, developing the Connor-Davidson Resilience Scale (CD-RISC). They emphasise the need for robust tools to quantify resilience, which is essential for empirical research and practical applications. Their work contrasts with more conceptual models, providing a standardised approach to assessing resilience (Connor and Zhang, 2006).

Bibliography

These references will provide further insights and a deeper understanding of resilience and well-being, aligning with the themes discussed in Chapter 5.

- Fletcher, D. and Sarkar, M. (2013) 'An integrative process model of resilience in an academic context: Resilience resources, coping strategies, and positive adaptation', PLOS ONE, 8(4), pp. e62948.
- Crawford, J., Butler-Henderson, K., Rudolph, J., and Glowatz, M. (2020) 'Stress adaptation and resilience of academics in higher education during the COVID-19 pandemic', Asia Pacific Education Review, 21(3), pp. 461-471.
- Li, W. and Hasson, F. (2020), 'Relationships between stress, burnout, mental health and well-being in nursing students', British Journal of Social Work, 54(2), pp. 668-684. Available at: https://academic.oup.com/bjsw/article/54/2/668/7379806.
- Martin, A.J. and Marsh, H.W. (2006), 'Academic resilience: underlying norms and validity of definitions', Educational Assessment, Evaluation and Accountability, 18(1), pp. 1-10.
- Connor, K.M. and Zhang, W. (2006), 'Resilience: Determinants, measurement, and treatment responsiveness', CNS Spectrums, 11(S12), pp. 5-12.

- Baek, J., Cho, Y. and Koo, W.W. (2009), 'The environmental consequences of globalization: A country-specific time-series analysis', Ecological Economics, 68(8–9), pp. 2255–2264.
- Leipold, B. and Greve, W. (2009), 'Resilience: A conceptual bridge between coping and development', European Psychologist, 14(1), pp. 40-50.

CHAPTER 6
Literature Review

Mindfulness, self-awareness, and resilience are critical aspects of psychological well-being that have garnered significant attention in academic literature. Various researchers have explored these concepts, offering insights into their mechanisms and implications for mental health, academic performance, and overall life satisfaction. This literature review compares and contrasts the views of different authors on these topics, drawing on the works of Damasio (1999), de Vibe et al. (2017), Dobkin, Bernardi, and Bagnis (2016), May et al. (2014), Morton, Helminen, and Felver (2020), Schonert-Reichl et al. (2015), Segal, Williams, and Teasdale (2018), Zenner, Herrnleben-Kurz, and Walach (2014), and Zimmaro et al. (2016).

Mindfulness, defined as "paying attention in a particular way: on purpose, in the present moment, and nonjudgmentally" (Bamber & Schneider, 2016), has been widely studied for its positive effects on mental health and cognitive functioning. Damasio (1999) provides a foundational understanding of the role of emotion and consciousness in mindfulness. He suggests that mindfulness practices enhance self-awareness and emotional regulation, leading to improved mental well-being.

De Vibe et al. (2017) conducted a randomised controlled trial demonstrating the long-term benefits of mindfulness-based interventions (MBIs) on medical and psychology students. Their findings indicate significant improvements in mindfulness, coping strategies, and overall well-being 6 years post-intervention. This study underscores the lasting impact of mindfulness training on psychological resilience.

Dobkin, Bernardi, and Bagnis (2016) highlight the dual benefits of mindfulness for both clinicians and patients. Their study emphasises how mindfulness enhances clinicians' well-being and patient-centred care, suggesting that mindfulness training should be integrated into healthcare education to improve the quality of care and clinician resilience.

May et al. (2014) conducted a meta-analysis on the association between mindfulness and academic performance, revealing a small but significant positive effect. They argue that mindfulness training can enhance executive functioning and working memory, which are critical for academic success. This view is supported by Zimmaro et al. (2016) who found that dispositional mindfulness is associated with lower stress levels and better well-being among university students.

Self-awareness, a component of mindfulness, is crucial for emotional regulation and psychological well-being. Schonert-Reichl et al. (2015) explored the impact of mindfulness training on elementary school students, finding significant improvements in executive functioning and working memory. Their study suggests that early mindfulness interventions can foster self-awareness and cognitive skills, leading to better academic and social outcomes.

Segal, Williams, and Teasdale (2018) in their work on mindfulness-based cognitive therapy (MBCT) emphasise the role of mindfulness in preventing depressive relapse. MBCT integrates mindfulness practices with cognitive therapy techniques to enhance self-awareness and emotional regulation, helping individuals recognise and respond to negative thought patterns.

Morton, Helminen, and Felver (2020) conducted a systematic review of mindfulness interventions on psychophysiological responses to acute stress. Their findings suggest that mindfulness practices reduce stress reactivity and enhance emotional regulation, supporting the view that mindfulness fosters self-awareness and resilience.

Resilience, the ability to adapt to stress and adversity, is closely linked to mindfulness and self-awareness. Zenner, Herrnleben-Kurz, and Walach (2014) conducted a systematic review and meta-analysis of mindfulness-based interventions in schools, finding that such interventions significantly improve students' resilience and academic performance. They argue that incorporating mindfulness into educational curricula can enhance students' ability to cope with stress and improve their overall well-being.

Zimmaro et al. (2016) also emphasise the role of mindfulness in enhancing resilience. Their study found that mindfulness practices are associated with lower perceived stress and better cognitive functioning, suggesting that mindfulness can buffer the negative effects of stress and promote resilience.

Dobkin, Bernardi, and Bagnis (2016) further support this view, highlighting how mindfulness training enhances clinicians' resilience, enabling them to provide better patient care. They argue that mindfulness should be a core component of healthcare education to promote clinician well-being and resilience.

Bibliography

Here is a bibliography of academic references related to the content of Chapter 6, which can serve as further reading for the readers:

- Bamber, M. D., & Schneider, J. K. (2016). Mindfulness-based programs and the American college student.

In Mindfulness, Self-Care, and Stress Management (pp. 207-218). Springer.

- Damasio, A. (1999). The feeling of what happens: Body and emotion in the making of consciousness. Houghton Mifflin Harcourt.
- de Vibe, M., Solhaug, I., Rosenvinge, J. H., Tyssen, R., Hanley, A., & Garland, E. (2017). Six-year positive effects of a mindfulness-based intervention on mindfulness, coping, and well-being in medical and psychology students; results from a randomized controlled trial. PLoS ONE, 12(4), e0176531.
- Dobkin, P. L., Bernardi, N. F., & Bagnis, C. I. (2016). Enhancing clinicians' well-being and patient-centered care through mindfulness. Journal of Continuing Education in the Health Professions, 36(1), 11-16.
- May, R. W., Seibert, G. S., Sanchez-Gonzalez, M. A., & Fincham, F. D. (2014). Meta-analysis of the association between mindfulness and academic performance. Frontiers in Psychology, 5, 603.
- Morton, M. L., Helminen, E. C., & Felver, J. C. (2020). A systematic review of mindfulness interventions on psychophysiological responses to acute stress. Mindfulness, 11, 2039-2054.
- Schonert-Reichl, K. A., Oberle, E., Lawlor, M. S., Abbott, D., Thomson, K., Oberlander, T. F., & Diamond, A. (2015). Enhancing cognitive and social-emotional development through a simple-to-administer mindfulness-based school program for elementary school children: A randomized controlled trial. Developmental Psychology, 51(1), 52-66.
- Segal, Z. V., Williams, J. M. G., & Teasdale, J. D. (2018). Mindfulness-based cognitive therapy for depression. Guilford Publications.

- Zenner, C., Herrnleben-Kurz, S., & Walach, H. (2014). Mindfulness-based interventions in schools – a systematic review and meta-analysis. Frontiers in Psychology, 5, 603.
- Zimmaro, L. A., Salmon, P., Naidu, H., Rowe, J., Phillips, K. & Rebholz, W. N. (2016). Association of dispositional mindfulness with stress, cortisol, and well-being among university undergraduate students. Mindfulness, 7(4), 874-885.

These references provide a comprehensive overview of the benefits of mindfulness, self-awareness and resilience, aligning well with the themes discussed in Chapter 6.

CHAPTER 7
Literature Review

The concept of happiness and well-being has been extensively studied across various disciplines, resulting in a multitude of perspectives. This literature review examines key contributions from prominent scholars, contrasting their viewpoints and highlighting areas of agreement and divergence.

Happiness and well-being are multifaceted constructs encompassing emotional, psychological and social dimensions. Diener (2009) provides a foundational framework by emphasising subjective well-being, which includes life satisfaction, the presence of positive emotions and the absence of negative emotions. This tripartite model has influenced subsequent research, underscoring the importance of both affective and cognitive evaluations of life.

In contrast, Huppert and So (2013) propose a broader definition of well-being, incorporating aspects of flourishing such as positive relationships, purpose, and personal growth. Their framework suggests that well-being extends beyond mere happiness to encompass a state of optimal functioning.

This perspective aligns with Seligman's (2011) PERMA model, which identifies 5 elements of well-being: Positive Emotions, Engagement, Relationships, Meaning, and Accomplishment.

The relationship between income and happiness has been a subject of considerable debate. Clark, Frijters, and Shields (2008) investigate this link, proposing the Easterlin paradox, which posits that beyond a certain income threshold, additional wealth has a negligible effect on happiness. They argue that relative income, or one's income compared to others, is a more significant determinant of well-being than absolute income.

Diener, Oishi, and Lucas (2003) further explore this paradox, finding that while wealthier individuals report higher life satisfaction, the impact of income on happiness diminishes over time. This attenuation effect suggests that once basic needs are met, factors such as relationships and personal achievements become more critical for sustained well-being.

The psychological perspective on well-being often emphasises the role of positive emotions and mental states. Fredrickson (2001) introduces the broaden-and-build theory, which posits that positive emotions expand cognitive and behavioural repertoires, leading to the development of enduring personal resources. This theory highlights the instrumental role of positive emotions in fostering resilience and well-being.

Philosophical approaches, such as those discussed by Huppert and So (2013), often focus on the ethical and normative aspects of well-being. These theories aim to identify the constitutive elements of a good life, such as virtue, meaning, and fulfilment. Integrating philosophical and psychological perspectives, Mitchell and Alexandrova (2021) argue for a meta-theoretical unification, suggesting that well-being encompasses both subjective experiences and objective conditions.

The significance of social relationships in promoting well-being is widely acknowledged. Sheldon and Lyubomirsky (2006) emphasise that sustainable increases in happiness are often achieved through intentional activities that enhance social connections, such as acts of kindness and expressing gratitude. Their research supports the notion that social bonds are crucial for emotional well-being.

Huppert and So (2013) extend this idea by incorporating positive relationships into their flourishing framework, underscoring the role of supportive social networks in achieving optimal functioning. Similarly, Seligman's (2011) PERMA model includes relationships as a core component, highlighting the interdependence of social connections and individual well-being.

Various strategies have been proposed to enhance well-being through cognitive and behavioural interventions. Lyubomirsky, King, and Diener (2005) advocate for positive activities, such as savouring experiences and practising optimism, as effective means to boost happiness. Their research demonstrates that such interventions can lead to lasting improvements in well-being.

Clark, Westergård-Nielsen, and Kristensen (2009) focus on the economic aspect, examining how economic satisfaction and income rank influence subjective well-being. They find that individuals' perceptions of their economic status relative to others significantly impact their happiness, suggesting that cognitive appraisals play a crucial role in well-being.

Diener et al. (2010) emphasise the importance of integrating different perspectives to develop a comprehensive understanding of well-being. They argue that combining subjective and objective measures can provide a more holistic view of what constitutes a good life. This integrative approach is reflected in the work of Fredrickson (2001) and Seligman

(2011), who blend psychological insights with broader philosophical considerations.

Huppert and So (2013) also advocate for a multidimensional approach, suggesting that well-being should be assessed across various domains, including emotional, psychological, and social dimensions. This perspective aligns with the growing consensus that well-being is a complex and multifaceted construct, requiring a nuanced and interdisciplinary approach.

Bibliography

These references provide a solid foundation for further exploration into the topics discussed in Chapter 7, including the nature of happiness, the benefits of positive emotions, and various approaches to enhancing well-being.

- Diener, E., Helliwell, J. F., & Kahneman, D. (Eds.), (2010), International Differences in Well-Being, Oxford University Press.
- Huppert, F. A., & So, T. T. C. (2013), Flourishing across Europe: Application of a new conceptual framework for defining well-being. Social Indicators Research, 110(3), 837-861.
- Lyubomirsky, S., King, L., & Diener, E. (2005). The benefits of frequent positive affect: Does happiness lead to success? Psychological Bulletin, 131(6), 803-855.
- Seligman, M. E. P. (2011). Flourish: A Visionary New Understanding of Happiness and Well-being. Free Press.
- Clark, A. E., Frijters, P., & Shields, M. A. (2008). Relative income, happiness, and utility: An explanation for the Easterlin paradox and other puzzles. Journal of Economic Literature, 46(1), 95-144.
- Dodge, R., Daly, A. P., Huyton, J., & Sanders, L. D. (2012). The challenge of defining wellbeing. International Journal of Wellbeing, 2(3), 222-235.

- Diener, E. (2009). Assessing subjective well-being: Progress and opportunities. In E. Diener (Ed.), Assessing Well-Being: The Collected Works of Ed Diener (pp. 11-58). Springer.
- Fredrickson, B. L. (2001). The role of positive emotions in positive psychology: The broaden-and-build theory of positive emotions. American Psychologist, 56(3), 218-226.
- Sheldon, K. M., & Lyubomirsky, S. (2006). Achieving sustainable gains in happiness: Change your actions, not your circumstances. Journal of Happiness Studies, 7(1), 55-86.
- Diener, E., Oishi, S., & Lucas, R. E. (2003). Personality, culture, and subjective well-being: Emotional and cognitive evaluations of life. Annual Review of Psychology, 54, 403-425.

Notes

Author Bio

Krishnan CA is on a mission to inspire individuals to achieve career success while balancing personal fulfilment.

Currently the SVP and Global Head at Tech Mahindra, he leads large deals and drives digital transformations. Previously, as a Business Unit Head at Tata Consultancy Services, he conceptualized innovative platforms that earned accolades like the **Tata Innovista and Best Large Deal awards.** With decades of experience across Fortune 500 clients in banking, telecom, manufacturing, and retail, Krishnan has secured **$3 Bn+ in deals** and received **60+ awards.**

An alumnus of IIM-A, Krishnan is a gold medalist in both MBA and Engineering and a recipient of the prestigious **Economic Times Young Leader Award.** A lifelong learner, Krishnan has also completed executive programs at **MIT, Columbia Business School, and INSEAD,** focusing on AI, Design Thinking, and Digital Transformation.

Blending corporate experience from his tenure at the TATA and Mahindra Group, with academic research and insights from the Bhagavad Gita, Krishnan empowers others to discover their purpose, realise their true potential, and lead lives enriched with **happiness, purpose, and impact.**

Krishnan welcomes reader feedback and can be reached at krishnan.c.a2004@gmail.com or https://www.linkedin.com/in/krishnanca/

www.ingramcontent.com/pod-product-compliance
Lightning Source LLC
Chambersburg PA
CBHW032013150726
47990CB00005B/1944